Exploring the Coast by Boat

**Puget Sound / San Juan Islands / Gulf Islands /
Vancouver Area / Upper Strait of Georgia /
Desolation Sound and Discovery Islands**

D0377379

Volume I

Dedication

to Michael
who took me adventuring in little boats

and to
Farrell, Tina, and Chantell
our valiant crew

Exploring
the Coast by Boat

**Puget Sound / San Juan Islands / Gulf Islands /
Vancouver Area / Upper Strait of Georgia /
Desolation Sound and Discovery Islands**

Frieda Van der Ree

Volume I

Edited by Gordon R. Elliott

Gordon Soules Book Publishers Ltd., Vancouver/London
The Writing Works, Seattle, Washington

First printing June, 1979
Second printing September, 1979
Third printing September, 1981
Fourth printing March, 1984

Canadian Cataloguing in Publication Data

Van der Ree, Frieda, 1943-
    Exploring the Coast by Boat

    Includes indexes.
    ISBN 0-919574-24-6 (v. 1)(Soules)
    ISBN 0-916076-09-1 (Writing Works)

    1. Boats and boating — British Columbia —
Guide-books. 2. Boats and boating —
Washington (State) — Guide-books. 3.
British Columbia — Description and travel —
1950-   —Guide-books. 4. Washington
(State) — Description and travel — Guide-
books. I. Title.
GV776.15.B7V35   797.1'0971'1   C78-002186-X

Library of Congress Catalog Card Number: 79-63559

Published in Canada, Britain, and the United States, as follows:

Gordon Soules Book Publishers Ltd.   **The Writing Works**
Canadian Address: Division of Morse Press, Inc.
C302 - 355 Burrard Street   417 East Pine Street
Vancouver, Canada V6C 2G6   Seattle, Washington
                                            U.S.A.   98122

British Address:
42/45 New Broad Street
London EC2 M1QY
England

Designed by Chris Bergthorson
Typeset by Domino-Link Word & Data Processing Ltd.
Printed and bound in Canada by Hignell Printing Limited

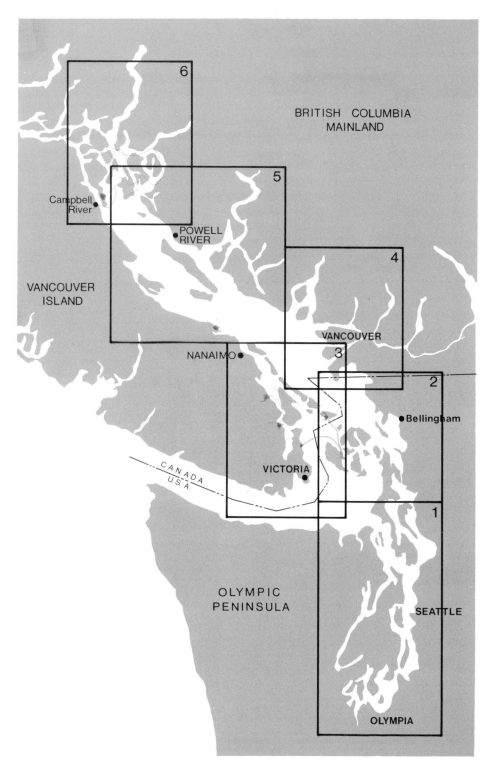

BRITISH COLUMBIA
MAINLAND

6

5

4

Campbell
River

POWELL
RIVER

VANCOUVER
ISLAND

VANCOUVER

NANAIMO

3

2

Bellingham

CANADA
U.S.A.

VICTORIA

1

OLYMPIC
PENINSULA

SEATTLE

OLYMPIA

Table of Contents

Chapter Five: Upper Strait of Georgia

Chapter Six: Desolation Sound and Discovery Islands

Acknowledgement

My thanks go to all those people who, individually, in boating associations, or in government offices on both sides of the border, annotated pages of the manuscript and answered my queries. And to the many people along the way who so willingly gave advice, information, instructions, and the benefit of their experiences. The list of all those who one way or another put in an oar to steer this book to completion would be a long one: my sincere thanks to each.

Some deserve special mention. Art Lightburn, who could not have known what he was getting into when he volunteered to do all the darkroom work for this book. Knud Bruun, neighbour and mechanic, who kept our boat engines doing what boat engines are supposed to do during the years of cruising that preceded this book. And my family, who gave encouragement, help of the most practical kinds, and breakfast in bed when it counted most.

Introduction

Sometimes for a day, sometimes for a week, sometimes for two months at a time, my husband, our three children and I explored the coastline of Puget Sound and the Strait of Georgia, under power and under sail, in summer and in winter, with boats small and medium. We ventured from Howe Sound to Desolation Sound with an old sixteen-foot lifeboat, a double-ender with a homemade mast and sail, camping on beaches and pushing off to shores which from a small slow boat seemed frighteningly far from home. From the relative comforts of our next vessel, a twenty-six-foot sailboat, we roamed among the Gulf Islands and the San Juans. And then with a diesel displacement cruiser we ranged from Puget Sound to Queen Charlotte Strait.

The fifty-one areas included in this book indicate some of the amazing variety we found. Each area is as easily reached by small boat as by the most luxurious yacht. Many are just as accessible to landlubbers. The areas chosen are so spaced along the coast that while one or two might make an interesting day trip or weekend jaunt, several strung together would give focus to a longer cruise.

Each chapter includes popular areas as well as those less frequented. Some offer sophisticated services like resorts and marinas, and others offer only rugged rocky shores and sandy beaches, calm coves, or exciting current passages. Some feature a unique attraction such as Butchart Gardens in Tod Inlet, others just a generally enticing combination of good fishing, swimming, and safe anchorage. Or the howl of wild wolves.

Endless discoveries to make on this beautiful and protected coast. Protected from the ravages of open ocean swells and winds by the Olympic Peninsula and Vancouver Island. Further protected by scores of islands of all sizes, and landforms of all shapes, all of which make a vast network of channels, bays, sounds, and inlets.

Protected water, but all water deserves respect. Enjoy exploring, but take care. Where you go and when you go along this coast should depend on your boat, your experience, and the latest marine weather forecast.

Exploring the Coast by Boat

Charts Chart portions, reproduced by permission of the U.S. National Ocean Survey and of the Canadian Hydrographic Service, are offered as guides only, and not for use in navigating. The old American chart numbering system appears in parentheses. Buy and use the most up-to-date charts, lists of lights and buoys, and tide and current tables. These and other NOA and Hydrographic Service publications are listed in free chart catalogues available at many marine supply stores or by writing to government agencies:

> Pacific Marine Center
> National Ocean Survey
> 1801 Fairview Ave. E.
> Seattle, WA 98102

> Canadian Hydrographic Service
> Department of Fisheries and the Environment
> 1230 Government Street
> Victoria, B.C. V8W 1Y4

Caution Cautions mentioned in each section do not by any means include all possible trouble spots in an area, but merely stress those that boaters mention repeatedly.

Bridges Only bridges with clearance less than 18 metres (about 58 feet) are listed. Bridge clearance in Canada is generally measured from Higher High Water, Large Tides; in the U.S., from Normal High Water. Know the height of your mast. Don't forget the antenna!

Public Tidelands Tidelands in B.C. are generally free to public access; in Washington many of them are privately owned. Respect riparian rights. Public beaches in Washington are currently being marked. *Your Public Beaches*, a series of free booklets, explains the marking system and includes maps and information about many public tidelands:

> Department of Natural Resources
> Marine Land Management Division
> Public Lands Building
> Olympia, WA 98504

Facilities Supplies, services and facilities listed are intended to give only a general idea of what to expect in an area. A more detailed account would soon be outdated and therefore would soon be misleading.

The shoreside state parks listed are those that offer mooring floats and/or mooring buoys, and some camping or at least picnic facilities. Various other agencies maintain public tidelands, parks, and shoreside access for the boating public. For an up-to-date listing of these, and for other information of interest to shoreside explorers, purchase the *Washington Marine Atlas*: Volume 1, North Inland Waters; Volume 2, South Inland Waters. $4.00 each from the Department of Natural Resources, Olympia.

Write for information about special events, accommodation, recreation and tourist attractions, maps, Chamber of Commerce Directory....

Department of Commerce and Economic Development
Travel Development Division
General Administration Building
Olympia, WA 98504

Ministry of the Provincial Secretary and Travel Industry
1117 Wharf Street
Victoria, B.C. V8W 2Z2

Seafood Restrictions Free booklets explain the current regulations and restrictions on taking fish and shellfish. The booklets are available at almost any marina or by writing to government departments:

Washington State Department of Fisheries
115 General Administration Building
Olympia, WA 98504

Marine Resources Branch
Ministry of Recreation and Conservation
1019 Wharf Street
Victoria, B.C. V8W 2Z1

Distances and Measurements Miles are nautical miles: 6080 feet rather than 5280 feet of the statute mile. Measurements, except in the recipes, are metric; conversions are approximations. For a table of conversions see page 149.

Chapter One
Puget Sound

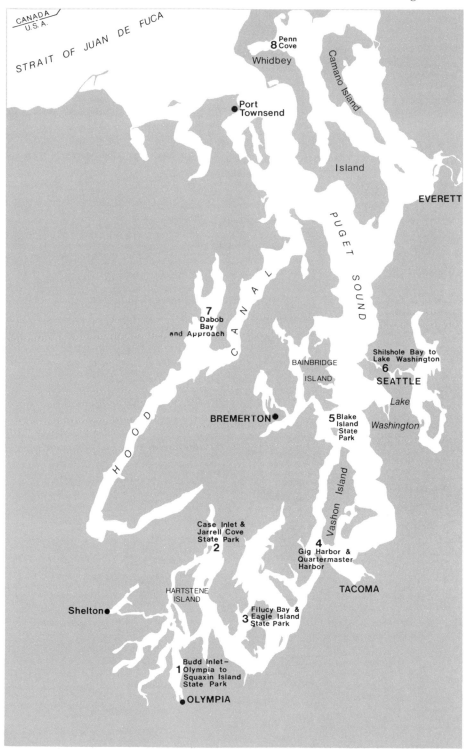

CANADA
U.S.A.

STRAIT OF JUAN DE FUCA

8 Penn Cove

Whidbey

Camano Island

Port Townsend

Island

EVERETT

PUGET SOUND

7 Dabob Bay and Approach

HOOD CANAL

Shilshole Bay to Lake Washington **6**

BAINBRIDGE ISLAND

SEATTLE

Lake

BREMERTON ●

5 Blake Island State Park

Washington

Vashon Island

Case Inlet & Jarrell Cove State Park **2**

4 Gig Harbor & Quartermaster Harbor

HARTSTENE ISLAND

TACOMA

Shelton ●

Filucy Bay & Eagle Island State Park **3**

Budd Inlet – Olympia to Squaxin Island State Park **1**

● OLYMPIA

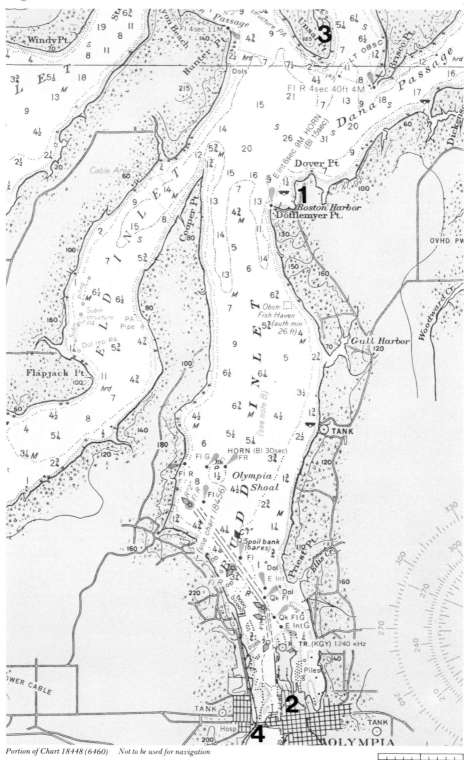

1 nautical mile

1

Budd Inlet — Olympia to Squaxin Island State Park

What's There Olympia oysters and Olympia beer....tours of the Legislative Buildings....harbourside restaurant with guest dock....brewery tours....marine park....

Charts
18445 (185-SC) small craft chart:

south Puget Sound and Hood Canal	1:80,000
inset of Budd Inlet	1:20,000
18456 (6462) Olympia Harbor and Budd Inlet	1:20,000

Moorage At Boston Harbor,[1] some marina moorage

Near Olympia,[2] marina moorage; anchorage in shallow water outside the marked traffic lanes

At Squaxin Island State Park,[3] mooring buoys, landing float at the public wharf, and good anchorage

Facilities At the village of Boston Harbor, some marine facilities and groceries

At Olympia, complete small craft marina services and tourist facilities

Squaxin Island State Park: 31 acres, campsites, pit toilets, tables; no drinking water

Caution Stay in the dredged, marked channel when approaching Olympia. The mud flats may dry at low tides, and the shallow water is foul with snags and piles.

Storm warnings are posted at the main dock at Olympia.

Access By car to most of the Budd Inlet shoreline; by boat only to Squaxin Island State Park

Launching ramps: Boston Harbor; Olympia

Olympia oysters and Olympia beer: no better combination. And no better reason for a cruise. Besides, Olympia is pleasantly walkable and handy to the harbourside.

The head of Budd Inlet is as far south as a cruising boat can go in Puget Sound, about 139 miles south of the International Boundary at Blaine. The inlet is really the back door to Olympia and the shores are green and wooded, a surprisingly undeveloped approach to a state capitol. The harbour channel, easy to navigate; wide, and deep enough to accommodate the deep-sea ships that stop for lumber.

But Olympia is a seaport only as a sideline. Its main business is government, and that is another attraction for the boating tourist. Capitol Lake[4] reflects grass and gardens and the stately old Legislative buildings. Inside, the buildings are studies in marble and Tiffany chandeliers, and the tour guides give a fascinating spiel: one chandelier weighs five tons and is large enough to hold a dinghy within it.

Some other worthwhile stops: find the Department of Natural Resources' office for some useful booklets of cruising information. And the State Museum, at Columbia and 21st Streets, displays rare finds from Puget Sound shorelines. A rusty hand gun, uncovered on Squaxin Island. Chinese jars. Indian artifacts. A petroglyph from Eld Inlet. And geological curiosities. A few blocks away, a lucky find is a used-book store selling pocket books for a dime apiece. Good rainy day reading on a boat. Puget Sound has its share of rainy days.

Even for non-beer drinkers a tour of the Olympia Brewery holds fascinations: steaming cauldrons, gleaming pipes, banks of pressure valves and dials. And for the beer drinkers, samples. The brewery is open to visitors from 0800 to 1630 each day, and a tour starts every fifteen minutes. The hike along Capitol Lake to Tumwater Falls is a fair one, but buses are available.

The little Olympia oysters, all but stripped from the public beaches, are still grown commercially in southern Puget Sound. These native oysters are becoming rare, but a treat worth buying to enjoy with the local beer.

Then for a change from city pace, Squaxin Island State Park: a quiet stopover with paths and gravel beach and acres of grassy field. Walk quietly, and you may surprise a grazing deer.

Marble arches and wild deer within an hour's cruising!

Did you know: A quart jar holds about 500 shucked Olympia oysters.

How to Put the Nip on an Olympia Oyster

Purists claim that the only way to enjoy an Olympia oyster is raw, on the half shell. With a twist of lemon.

If, like me, you are not a purist, poach the oysters first: simmer them about 2 minutes in salted water until they firm up. Then chill and serve as though they were raw. With or without sauce. A nippy sauce really puts an exclamation point behind the delicate oyster flavour.

Nippy Oyster Dipping Sauce

½ cup of ketchup
Juice of one lemon
A few drops of tabasco
Shake together in a jar

State Capitol overlooking moorage at Olympia

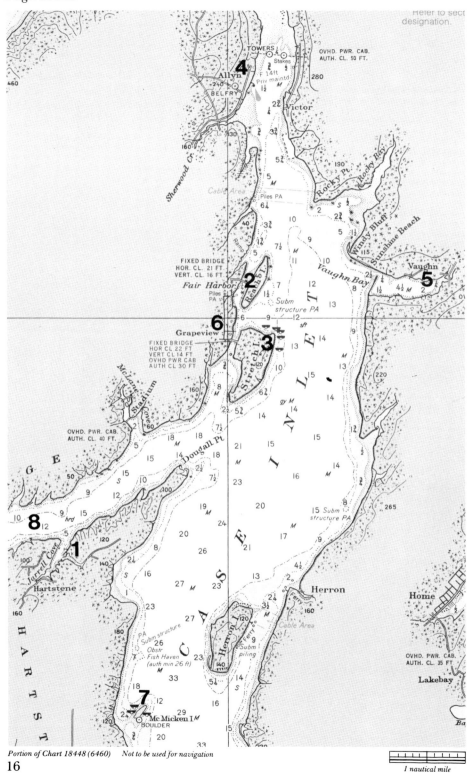

1 nautical mile

NANAIMO

VANCOUVER

VICTORIA

Strait of Juan De Fuca

PORT
ANGELES

Everett

Puget
Sound

SEATTLE

Olympia

2

Case Inlet and Jarrell Cove State Park

What's There many public beaches....good year-round fishing....small shoreline communities....farms and orchards and vineyards....small-boat camping....quiet, scenic passages....winery museum tour....

Charts
18445 (185-SC) small craft chart:
      south Puget Sound and Hood Canal   1:80,000
18448 (6460) Puget Sound: Seattle to Olympia   1:80,000

Moorage Jarrell Cove:[1] mooring floats and buoys at the state park and a marina dock

    Grapeview[6] vicinity: moorage at the marina at Fair Harbor[2] and mooring buoys at Stretch Point State Park[3]

    Excellent anchorage in a choice of bays and coves

Facilities Some general supplies at the villages of Allyn,[4] Vaughn,[5] and Grapeview[6]

    Marina and camping facilities, and groceries, at Jarrell Cove and at Fair Harbor

    Jarrell Cove State Park: 43 acres, bathhouse with hot showers, campsites, tables, trails, grassy clearing

Caution Sailboats approaching from Pickering Passage[8] note that a fixed highway bridge with a clearance of 9.5 metres (31 feet) spans the passage.

    Watch for the drying rock in Fair Harbor.

Access Hartstene Island is connected to the mainland by a highway bridge over Pickering Passage. Car access to Jarrell Cove State Park and to many points along Case Inlet; by boat only to Stretch Point State Park

    Launching ramps: Fair Harbor; Allyn; Vaughn Bay

Ever dreamed of cruising past romantic shores? Try cruising Case Inlet. Orchards and vineyards suggest why Puget Sound has been called the Mediterranean of the West. Beautiful in spring, when the orchards are in bloom.

Stretch Island was once named Isle of Grapes and the winery there is now a museum, with tours given by the owner. Nearby Stretch Point State Park is a sand and gravel dune that traps a natural salt-water aquarium — for strange skittering bugs and shaggy grasses, and other queer "things" that you don't really want to wade through, no matter how temptingly warm the water may be. The park is a good picnic spot: drift logs as comfortable seats, and a fine view down Case Inlet.

What can't be found in this part of Puget Sound seems hardly worth looking for. Beaches, clean and curved and sandy. More important, many beaches are public and marked as such. Salmon and cutthroat trout and bottom fish. Scuba diving by the artificial reef north of McMicken Island.[7] And gunkholing — the best! Bays and bights and little coves, all in sheltered water.

Jarrell Cove, with its forested state park on one shore and a small tree-shaded marina on the other, is perfectly self-contained for small-boat camping. At the park some campsites overlook the beach; others face morning sunshine and an old orchard in acres of trimmed field. Showers, laundry facilities, and a bottle of wine with a freshly caught fish — all available without leaving the cove.

Curiously, the two park wharves, only a few hundred feet apart, appear to be in totally different climates. One wharf is shaded by tall evergreens; the other faces pines and arbutus on a wind-blasted bluff. Inland along the park trails it's raincoast forest again, all sword fern and salal. And against this dark green background, a single perfect tiger lily, a shock of exotic orange!

Did you know: Tiger lilies were a food plant for the Indians who steamed and ate the bulbs.

A Case of Inlet Names

Some place names in Case Inlet speak for themselves, some speak of long gone people.

Rocky Point, Windy Bluff, Sunshine Beach, all self-explanatory. Fair Harbor is fair indeed, if you avoid the rock between Reach Island and the mainland. Grapeview, overlooking the Isle of Grapes, was originally named Detroit! The Isle of Grapes is really Stretch Island. Reach Island is also called Treasure Island. Was the treasure ever reached?

The Wilkes exploring expedition of 1841 established most of the names around the inlet. Case was a lieutenant. Pickering an ethnologist. Samuel Stretch, a gunner's mate. And because Lieutenant Henry J. Hartstene's name was so variously spelled on the ship's roster, the island has been designated over the last century as Hartstein, Hartstine, Harstine and Harstene.

W.D. Vaughn had been a pioneer: a fighter in the Indian wars and a hunter of renown, and finally a settler at Case Inlet. He lost his pre-emption during an illness, but the district that took his land kept his name.

Calm moorage at Jarrell Cove

Gravel shores and driftwood at Eagle Island

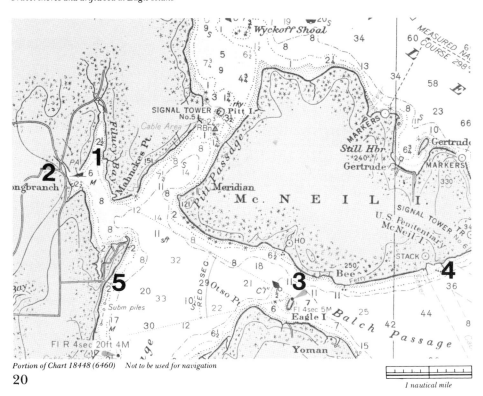

Portion of Chart 18448 (6460)   Not to be used for navigation

1 nautical mile

3

Filucy Bay and Eagle Island State Park

What's There an island to walk around....good salmon fishing....small village....secure anchorage....clam digging....beachcombing....federal penitentiary on McNeill Island....

Charts
18445 (185-SC) small craft chart:
    south Puget Sound and Hood Canal   1:80,000
18448 (6460) Puget Sound: Seattle to Olympia   1:80,000

Moorage In Filucy Bay,[1] very sheltered anchorage, and temporary visitors' moorage at the Longbranch Improvement Club Dock[2]
    Mooring buoys at Eagle Island State Park[3]

Facilities At Longbranch, some general supplies and limited marina facilities
    Eagle Island State Park: 10 acres, undeveloped

Caution When tied to a mooring buoy at Eagle Island watch for changing water depths: the buoys swing toward shallow water at low tide and with the currents.
    Steer carefully clear of Eagle Island Reef, which is marked by a buoy on its northwest side and by the red sector of a light on the north tip of Eagle Island.

Note: Signs on the shore of McNeill Island warn unauthorized boats to stay away from the penitentiary area.[4]

Access By car to Longbranch; by boat only to Eagle Island
    Launching ramp: outside Filucy Bay[5]

Bull kelp winding around the mooring buoys; the water clear; on shore, nothing but beach and trees and one weathered picnic table: Eagle Island is a good place for the quiet, simple elements of a cruise.

Beachcomb a low-tide wilderness of salt-bleached barnacles and patches of blue mussels. Small crabs hide under the waterline rocks with tiny eels, hermit crabs, and whelks. Ragged sea lettuce grows in the shallows along with all sorts of squirty, squishy "things". You may dig up some clams, but do you have to? They are becoming so scarce around here.

Walk right around the island when the tide isn't full, or cross the island on trails through its topknot of evergreen and arbutus. Eagle Island is barely ten acres, and shrinking because of waves and currents nibbling at the shore. Because of erosion a ragged row of undercut trees leans onto the beach and the concrete base of a navigation light has dropped to the shingle. The light on the bluff above will soon, again, be moved away from the edge.

The edges of the island fall in chunks onto the beach which the waves rearrange into patches of sand and gravel, just enough of each to build a very respectable sand castle without actually having to sit on sand. Sand is fun, but gravel is clean.

Birds — what kinds? — scuttle across the beach and seem to disappear into the clay-and-gravel cliffs: the clay is riddled with bird-size burrows.

Nearby Filucy Bay is wonderfully protected from all winds, and Longbranch is handy for picking up a few groceries or some ice. The community could be a western movie set: hot quiet streets with weeds, people drifting around, buzzing blue bottle flies, and in the store, "wanted" posters.

Did you know: Rockfish spines contain a poison which may cause a very painful wound. To handle rockfish safely, snip the tips off the spines. Wire cutters do the job nicely.

State Marine Parks in Puget Sound

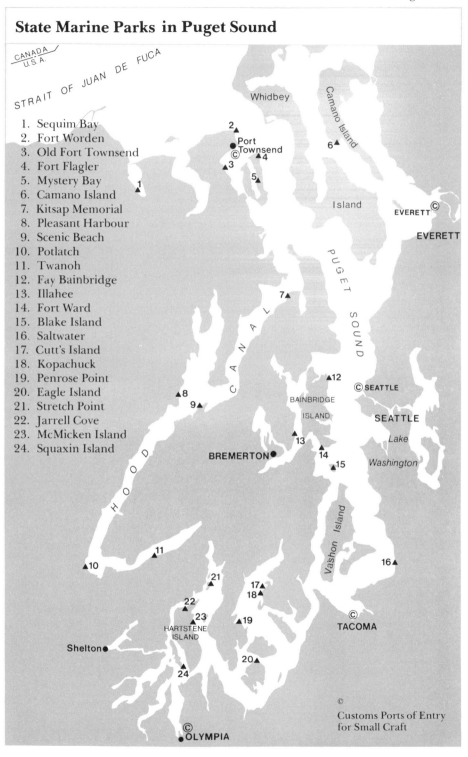

CANADA
U.S.A.

STRAIT OF JUAN DE FUCA

1. Sequim Bay
2. Fort Worden
3. Old Fort Townsend
4. Fort Flagler
5. Mystery Bay
6. Camano Island
7. Kitsap Memorial
8. Pleasant Harbour
9. Scenic Beach
10. Potlatch
11. Twanoh
12. Fay Bainbridge
13. Illahee
14. Fort Ward
15. Blake Island
16. Saltwater
17. Cutt's Island
18. Kopachuck
19. Penrose Point
20. Eagle Island
21. Stretch Point
22. Jarrell Cove
23. McMicken Island
24. Squaxin Island

Whidbey

Camano Island

Port Townsend

Island

EVERETT

EVERETT

PUGET SOUND

H O O D   C A N A L

SEATTLE

BAINBRIDGE ISLAND

SEATTLE

Lake

BREMERTON

Washington

Vashon Island

Shelton

HARTSTENE ISLAND

TACOMA

Customs Ports of Entry
for Small Craft

OLYMPIA

23

The backdrop to busy Gig Harbor is spectacular Mount Rainier

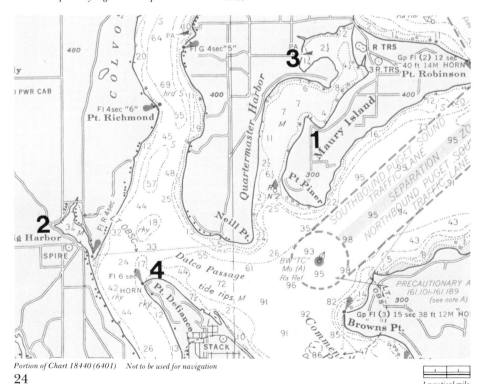

Portion of Chart 18440 (6401)   Not to be used for navigation

24

1 nautical mile

4

Gig Harbor and Quartermaster Harbor

What's There two sheltered harbours....rambles on country roads....excellent fishing....wild mushrooms....a county park for boaters....waterside taverns and restaurants....boutiques and galleries....

Charts

18445 (185-SC) small craft chart:	
south Puget Sound and Hood Canal	1:80,000
inset of Gig Harbor	1:20,000
18448 (6460) Puget Sound: Seattle to Olympia	1:80,000

Moorage Secure anchorage in both harbours, but watch for shoal water at the head of each: check depths before anchoring

Visitors' moorage at marinas in Gig Harbor[2] and at Burton[3] in Quartermaster Harbor

Landing floats at Dockton County Park[1] in Quartermaster Harbor

Facilities At Gig Harbor, all cruising supplies, and marina and tourist services

At Burton, in Quartermaster Harbor, a marina and some general supplies

Dockton County Park: bathhouse with hot showers, marked swim area, covered cooking pits, a general store nearby

Caution A sand bar on the east side, marked by a light, constricts the entrance to Gig Harbor. Take account of currents when entering or leaving, and watch for other boats.

Storm warnings are posted at Point Defiance.[4]

Access Car access to both harbours. Car ferries to northern Vashon Island from Point Southworth and to southern Vashon Island from Point Defiance (Tacoma)

Launching ramps: Dockton County Park; Gig Harbor; Burton

Gig and Quartermaster: two harbours for two kinds of cruising moods. Nicely nautical names within six miles of each other, and near some of the finest fishing in Puget Sound.

Gig Harbor is bustling and hustling, a supply centre for pleasure craft and home port to a fishing fleet. A good place to eat out, with guest docks at an elegant dress-up restaurant or at a lively informal tavern. And other restaurants, cafes and taverns just short walks away.

The town is very old and makes the most of its oldness: a buccaneer lurching down a back alley wouldn't seem out of place. The shops are small and very specialized; some fascinating browsing. Buy a driftwood windchime, pecan crunch ice cream, or an ancient anchor. Fun.

Quartermaster Harbor is a "seahorse" on the chart, with Burton at the mouth. A counterclockwise maze of harbour within harbour; good anchorage almost anywhere you care to drop a hook. Houses line the shore, but they aren't conspicuous, leaving space for the natural elements of the island to show through: sand cliffs, and forests of Douglas fir and manzanita. A low-key anchorage.

Dockton County Park, with its constant entertainment of wild ducks, schools of shiners, and lavish spread of sand, is an ideal children's playground. The swim area is roped off for safety and in summer patrolled by a lifeguard.

Dockton is neatly wrapped up in one village store which is also the post office and the gas station. This was once a boom town! A good place for walking: the roads are paved and the people are friendly. In berry season: blueberries, huckleberries, boysenberries and salmonberries, all by one short stretch of road. And mushrooms, mushrooms, mushrooms.

An old timer walking by invited us to help ourselves to the ripe cherries on a roadside tree. While we picked, he told wonderful stories about Dockton's past. The local history was surely his. But were the cherries?

Did you know: In 1825 Dockton was one of the busiest drydocks in Puget Sound, but by 1900 a ghost town. Strange things can be found where ships dropped their ballast in the harbour: seashells from exotic beaches, Chinese pottery and petrified teredo wood....

Something to Try: Hunting Edible Mushrooms

Puget Sound is a paradise for mushroom hunters. Wild mushrooms happen here in an incredible array of colour, form and size, and are as fascinating as their names: Golden Trumpets, Shaggy Manes, Angel Wings, Man on Horseback. The trick is to match names and mushrooms, for while dozens of species are deliciously edible, many are not, and a few are appallingly poisonous.

Identify a mushroom by the shape and colour of its cap and underparts, by its flesh and stem, and by the colour of its spore. Best to learn only one or two species at a time, with the help of someone really familiar with them. Or buy a good field guide and eat only the mushrooms that you can identify beyond a doubt.

Then try wild mushrooms fried with fresh-caught trout, all buttery mellow. Or when the fishing lines are empty, the mushrooms gently sautéed and sauced with sherry, served on toast. Then the trout is hardly missed at all.

Shaggy Mane

Coprinus comatus (black spores)

Colour and Description

Cap: white and gray covered with fluffy scales, standing erect like a closed umbrella on its handle, spreading with age, four to twelve inches in height; flesh white at first, then darkening.

Gills: white shading to pink, in flat folds against the stem, turning black with spores and melting into a black fluid.

Stem: white, hollow with small movable ring, slightly thicker at the base, four to ten inches in length.

When and Where Found

Spring or fall after rain; in the open, on the ground, in gravel by roadsides, near garbage dumps, or in decaying sawdust near old logging roads.

Remarks

A well-known, edible mushroom of good flavour and consistency if gathered when young. Easily distinguished from the similar inky cap by its height and fluffy scales.

by Margaret McKenny
from *The Savory Wild Mushroom*
Reprinted with permission
from the University of
Washington Press

shaggy mane

Puget Sound

At Tillicum Village, Blake Island

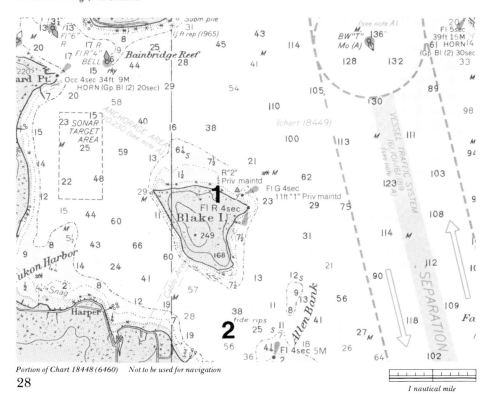

Portion of Chart 18448 (6460)   Not to be used for navigation

1 nautical mile

5

Blake Island State Park

What's There good small-boat camping....almost-tame deer....self-guiding trails....scuba diving....Tillicum Village....salmon barbecue....

Charts
18445 (185-SC) small craft chart:
      south Puget Sound and Hood Canal   1:80,000
18448 (6460) Puget Sound: Seattle to Olympia   1:80,000

Moorage Mooring buoys at several points around the island
    Floats behind a breakwater at Tillicum Village[1]

Facilities At Tillicum Village, a unique concession in a state park, salmon barbecue, native interpretive dancing, crafts and souvenirs
    Blake Island State Park: campsites, picnic tables, restrooms with hot showers, covered cook areas, group shelters
    Nearest complete marina facilities at Shilshole Bay (Seattle) about 8 miles to the northeast

Caution With a flooding current and strong south winds, heavy tide rips may form at the entrance to Colvos Pasasage.[2]
    Take care when approaching the moorage at Tillicum Village: the floats are reached by navigating a dredged, marked channel through shallow water.
    Storm warnings for this part of Puget Sound are posted at Shilshole Bay and at Des Moines.

Access By boat only; excursion boat from downtown Seattle to Tillicum Village, phone 322-6444

Blake Island, all 476 acres of it, is easy to reach from almost anywhere in Puget Sound. Perfect for a spur-of-the-moment cruise — with variety.

For a quiet weekend with a touch of wilderness, tie up to a mooring buoy near the point facing Colvos Passage. The current here swirls through jungles of bull kelp, and the island shore is rocky and forested. Yet for all the seeming remoteness, Seattle is only five miles away.

For a beach, with open space to wander and perhaps to build a bonfire when the sun goes down, the west side of the island is best. Here the island tapers along a gentle shore, an inviting sweep of sand and pebbles. Arbutus bark clatters down to the picnic tables, and wide, winding trails lead across the island and along the waterfront.

The chart indicates that the water off the northwest point of the island is a scuba diving area. Certainly clear water for underwater sightseeing, even in summer, and even from a drifting dinghy. The shore falls away in deepening steps. Six metres (20 feet), and you can still see crabs hiding in the eelgrass, and a dogfish rounding up a school of sandlance.

Maybe you prefer something more developed: moorage behind a breakwater, acres of grass, water on tap. And fire pits and barbecue pits, with a stock of firewood handy. Even rain shelters big enough for groups of people. All on the north side of Blake Island, facing the Seattle skyline.

Here, too, you'll find Tillicum Village. Not at every state park can you dine on barbecued salmon, and in a "longhouse" large enough to seat a thousand. Strange to see the land tourists in evening dress lined up to eat with boaters in shorts.

Blake Island supports a herd of over sixty deer, and the grassy fields near the longhouse tempt them into easy camera range. Some deer are tame enough to touch.

Did you know: Blake Island is thought to be the birthplace of Chief Sealth, after whom Seattle was named.

For Those Wrenching Engine Problems....

A dead battery, when you're anchored in a secluded inlet. A seized water pump, when you're fighting a malicious chop and the wind promises worse to come. A bent prop, when you're miles from the nearest marina. While foul weather spoils many a boating holiday, engine problems work up a livelier frustration; weather can't be helped, but things mechanical can be — though only if you have the parts, the tools, and the know-how.

Consider carrying the following items applicable to your engine type:
>fuel filters
>fuses
>pull cord for manual start outboards
>propeller
>shear pins
>spare battery and/or jumper cables
>spark plugs and spark plug wrench
>water pump impeller
>vee-belts

Some handy tools:
>Allen wrenches
>crescent wrench
>hammer
>screwdrivers
>water pump pliers
>vise grip pliers

For extended trips, especially those to remote waterways, consult a mechanic about a more extensive inventory of spare parts, tools and back-up systems. Add a flashlight to your toolbox. And for that time when all else fails, a long and sturdy towing line.

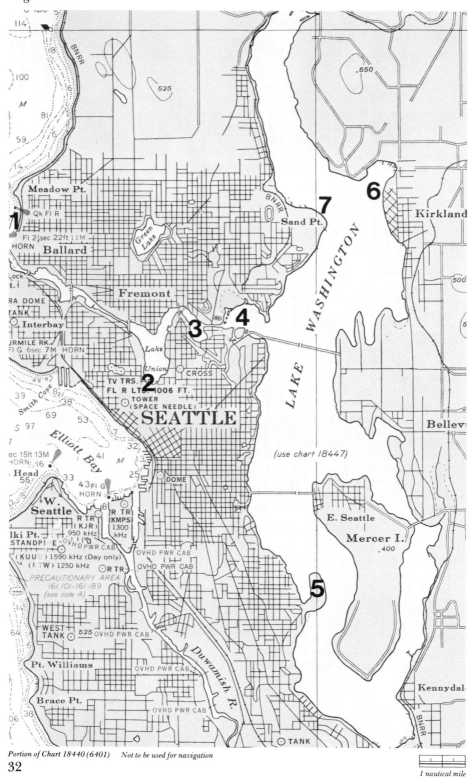

1 nautical mile

6

Shilshole Bay to Lake Washington

What's There fresh-water boating for sea-going boats....shoreline sightseeing tour of beautiful homes and lakeshore parks....museum ships' tour....salmon spawning streams....locks....hydroplane races....

Charts
18447 (690-SC) small craft chart:

Lake Washington Ship Canal	1:10,000
Lake Washington	1:25,000

Moorage Visitors' moorage at many marinas from Shilshole Bay[1] to Lake Washington

At Kirkland,[6] 48-hour visitors' moorage at the municipal wharf
Anchorage at various nooks and crannies

Facilities Everything imaginable!

Bridges entering from Shilshole Bay:

Great Northern railway bridge, clearance 13.1 metres (43 feet); signal to open:1 long 1 short

Ballard Bridge, 14 metres (46 feet); 1 long 1 short

Northern Pacific railway bridge, 4.6 metres (15 feet); 1 long 3 short

Fremont Avenue Bridge, 9.5 metres (31 feet); 1 long 1 short
University Bridge, 14 metres (46 feet); 1 long 3 short
Montlake Bridge, 14 metres (46 feet); 1 long 1 short

Note: Signs along the shores include permissible speeds within the canal and near the lakeshore. Boat wash can damage shoreline structures.

Access By car, to many points along the canal and lake
Launching ramps: many, at marinas and lakeside parks

Ever been through these locks before? First, scramble for a place along the retaining wall on the right side of the channel to wait your turn. Signal lights flash green for the next batch of boats to enter the locks. You might be lucky. Hectic moments then, while you fasten lines and fenders, and the attendants shout orders. Finally the lock gates close and you are at the bottom of a well. Water surges in all at once, and all together, almost as one, the boats rise smoothly. In ten minutes the gates open to the Lake Washington Ship Canal, and you are on the top of the world — 6.4 metres (21 feet) above sea level.

A fish ladder with viewing windows bypasses the locks to let salmon through to their fresh-water spawning streams. During a run hundreds of salmon mass, mill and jump among the boats in the lock approach. An incredible sight!

The ship canal links together a series of bays from the locks to Lake Washington: harbour, thoroughfare, commercial basin, waterfront parks, city. First, Lake Union[2] bellies to the south, toward the Space Needle, Seattle's famous landmark. Mooch around to find your own anchorage. Ours was temporary, just a few blocks from Seattle Centre, in a small basin among weeping willows, lily pads and mallard ducks. The Centre is a seventy-four-acre urban park with fountains, gardens, theatres, shops and amusements. Board the monorail and be in downtown Seattle within ninety seconds!

Portage Bay,[3] next, holds entire communities of floating homes and two yacht clubs; and then Union Bay,[4] on a sunny day a green space full of sailing dinghies and canoes. The University of Washington borders the north side of Union Bay, and the Arboretum lines the south side, accessible only to small, shallow-draft vessels.

Lake Washington is sixteen miles long: a lot of shoreline. All scenic in a finished way: Lake Washington is a city lake after all. Landscaped waterfront yards and landscaped parks. Public beaches, launching ramps, yacht clubs and private floats. A marina here and there. But mostly houses: rows and rows of houses rising in terraces around the lake.

Lake water is soothingly soft. Nice to swim in and boats soon lose their rime of salt. The lake is much cleaner now than five years ago: better sewage treatment, and a holding tank law.

Water skiers, scuba divers, dinghy sailors and canoeists also enjoy the lake, and for all of them, a variety of attractions. The hydroplane races. Bailey Peninsula,[5] with its beaches and walks, and its fish hatchery open to visitors. The three Museum Ships at Kirkland.[6] And across the lake from Kirkland, Sand Point Park,[7] with picnic tables and a landing dock.

Anchored in the lee of Sand Point, watch the sun setting on massive Mount Rainier and a gaff-rigged schooner slipping quietly across the coloured sky. What more does a cruise require?

Did you know: About thirty-six species of fish inhabit Lake Washington.

Using the Locks:

Obey instructions from lock signal lights, posted signs, and lock attendants.

Within 61 metres (200 feet) of the lock gates, reduce boat speed to a crawl, and enter the lock at dead slow speed.

Boats require two lines at least 15.2 metres (50 feet long), one fore, one aft, and two people on board to handle these lines.

Fender well to protect your boat from the lock walls and from other boats within the confined lock space.

Lift spans on Lake Washington Ship Canal

Hiram M. Chittenden Locks: gateway to fresh-water cruising

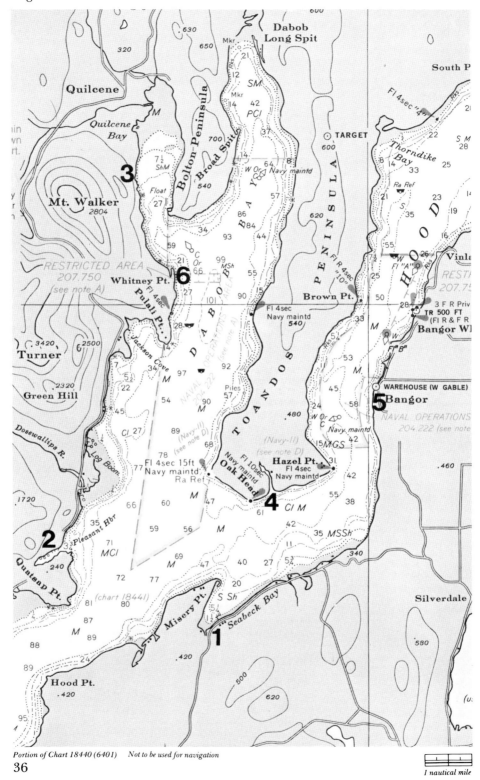

1 nautical mile

7

Dabob Bay and Approach

What's There seafood foraging....shellfish laboratory....hole-in-the-shore coves....nearby Olympia National Park....quiet, undeveloped shorelines....submarines and rhododendrons....

Charts

18445 (185-SC) small craft chart:
    south Puget Sound and Hood Canal   1:80,000
18458 (6422) Hood Canal: South Point to Quatsap Point
    including Dabob Bay   1:25,000

Moorage Marina slips at Seabeck[1] and at Pleasant Harbor;[2] at Quilcene Boat Haven,[3] some floats behind a breakwater

A state park wharf with floats at Pleasant Harbor

Good anchorage, especially in Pleasant Harbor and in Fisherman Harbor[4] for boats able to clear the shallow entrance

Facilities Seabeck: marina with fishing supplies and charts; store, cafe, picnic and campsites; boat rentals

Pleasant Harbor: marina with store, book-trade shelf, laundry and showers; a small state park (0.8 acre) with pit toilets

Quilcene Boat Haven: gasoline, showers

Caution Several areas in Dabob Bay and Hood Canal are designated U.S. Navy Operating Areas. Look for details on the charts, and in *United States Coast Pilot 7*.

Attempt the entrance to Fisherman Harbor only on a high and flooding tide. After crossing the spit, turn left and follow the spit almost to the shore, then turn toward deeper water near the centre of the harbour.

Access Car access to all the numbered points, and to many other parts of the Dabob Bay shore as well

Launching ramps: Seabeck; Quilcene Boat Haven; Whitney Point

The barb of fish-hook-shaped Hood Canal just barely misses piercing through to Puget Sound. And its not being part of Puget Sound makes all the difference. Hood Canal is a little more scenic, a little more isolated, a little more wild than are the cruising waters to the east. But paradoxically, at Bangor[5] it harbours an atomic submarine base.

Hood Canal means, most of all, seafood foraging. Salmon in all seasons. Clams of all kinds, from littlenecks to the giant geoducks. Red rock crabs and Dungeness crabs. Shrimp, mussels, scallops and cockles. Oysters. And bottom fish, of course.

All these near Dabob Bay, and some cruising amenities as well. Seabeck is only a few miles by road from urban centres. And most boats can enter Pleasant Harbor, which describes itself, at any tide, though the entrance is narrow. Fisherman Harbor, the navigator's challenge: its entrance comes close to drying at low tide, but inside the bottom drops away again to a respectable depth for anchoring.

Beautiful to snorkel here on a warm day. Or just drift over the shallows in a dinghy, and look down on the clouds of sea perch, and the hermit crabs hiding in the eel grass. And beds of oyster shells and dog whelks, their every curve and convolution clear even in 3 metres (10 feet) of water.

The gravel spit tipped with drift logs makes a good place to roast a day's shellfish taken from the public beaches. For good measure, a wealth of berries on the shore side of the spit, and a wild hazelnut tree half hidden among the Oregon grape and rhododendron.

Dabob Bay is warmer than most other parts of Puget Sound — good news for swimmers, and for oysters. Notice the stacks of shells, blindingly white in the sun, near oyster farms. At Whitney Point[6] the Department of Fisheries operates a shellfish laboratory, with outdoor displays for visitors and free information sheets available at the office. A fascinating afternoon stop.

Not so easy to reach, Quilcene is barred by a mile of mudflats and shallows, but if you really want to go there, moor behind the little breakwater on the western shore and walk to town. It's over a mile to walk, but who could resist even that to be on Linger Longer Road?

Did you know: Hood Canal is one of the best places to see shoreside displays of rhododendrons, Washington's state flower, blooming from May to July.

Launching ramp at Washington State Shellfish Laboratory at Whitney Point

rhododendron

"Colourful" Coupeville at Penn Cove, Whidbey Island

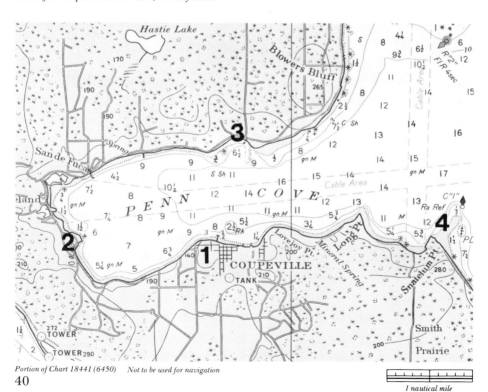

Portion of Chart 18441 (6450)   *Not to be used for navigation*

1 nautical mile

8

Penn Cove

What's There historic sites....museums....antiques....an old-fashioned inn with guest moorage....dry sunny climate....prairie rambles....

Charts

18423 (184-SC) small craft chart:
     Bellingham to Everett including San Juan Islands   1:80,000
18441 (6450) Admiralty Inlet and Puget Sound to Seattle   1:80,000

Moorage Good anchorage in Penn Cove
     Some float space at the Coupeville Wharf[1]
     Guest moorage at the Captain Whidbey Inn[2] for boats with less than 1.5 metres (5 feet) draft

Facilities Tourist attractions and tourist facilities at Coupeville[1]
     More complete cruising and boating services at nearby Oak Harbor

Caution Watch for Snatelum Point Spit[4] and the wreck there.

Access Car access to Whidbey Island via Deception Pass Bridge, or by car ferry from Mukilteo (near Everett) to the south end of Whidbey Island
     Launching ramps: Coupeville City Park one mile east of Coupeville; Penn Cove Park[3]

Coupeville, an island town in real rolling prairie, a seaside town, a county seat, and an Historic District. For any of these reasons, a fascinating place to visit.

A delightful place to wander through if you like to browse in antique shops, in gift-and-souvenir stores, and in little taverns and cafes. The museum brims with wonderful old things including a good collection of newspaper clippings and photographs, one of Deception Pass before the bridge was built.

Behind the old town and out of sight are the newer shops and buildings. Ninety buildings in the district are registered Historic Sites, most of these in Coupeville. Even the Coupeville wharf, built about 1900. It was known to be "safe landing at any tide" for steamers coming to Penn Cove, and though landing here is still safe at any tide a sign warns that you walk on the wharf at your own risk. A worthwhile risk. Through the gaps between the aged planks look down on congeries of starfish, and on the pilings shaggy with blue mussels. The perfect place to lie, stomach-down, to jig for piling perch and bass.

Out of the town and beyond it, the fields and flats of Ebeys Prairie and Smith Prairie. Lovely, gently rolling country. Good for walking. Good cycling too, for those finding space for bicycles on their boats.

Toward the head of Penn Cove, the Captain Whidbey Inn, built in 1907, is probably less changed than most of the other buildings. You can put up for the night or drop in for a meal or a bowl of chowder at this large and rambling inn fittingly constructed of madrona (arbutus) logs.

On few shores are there such masses of those lovely trees.

Did you know: In the early days everyone came to Whidbey Island by boat. One settler built a house at Coupeville, rowed across to Utsalady on Camano Island to collect his family and all their belongings, and rowed them back to their new home. Eight nautical miles each way!

About Arbutus

An extraordinary tree with eccentric habits, the only broad-leaf evergreen native to Canada, the arbutus keeps its leaves but sheds its bark.

Arbutus grows in solitary bushes, stunted and twisting; it grows fifteen metres tall and more in dense, proud, stands. Variety in form, variety in name as well: sometimes arbutus, sometimes madrona, or madrone. A close relation, the manzanita is usually redder, scalier, more bush-like and more crooked. All are members of the heather family and close cousins to the rhododendron, as a comparison of leaves will show.

The bark is dry and thin, peeling back in brittle parchment pieces. A chain mail clatter on a windy day. Indians steeped arbutus leaves and bark in boiling water to brew a cure for stomach-ache. Deer nibble the leaves of the tree, and birds eat the berries. Although arbutus is rarely used commercially, the wood is hard enough for turning and carving, and the bark could be used for tanning leather.

For boaters, enough that the trees decorate the shore so nicely. White flowers in spring. Leaves dark and glossy. The surprising orange-red of wood where the bark has peeled away. The pistachio green of young growth. And the bright red winter berries. A decoration all year round.

arbutus

Chapter Two
San Juan Islands

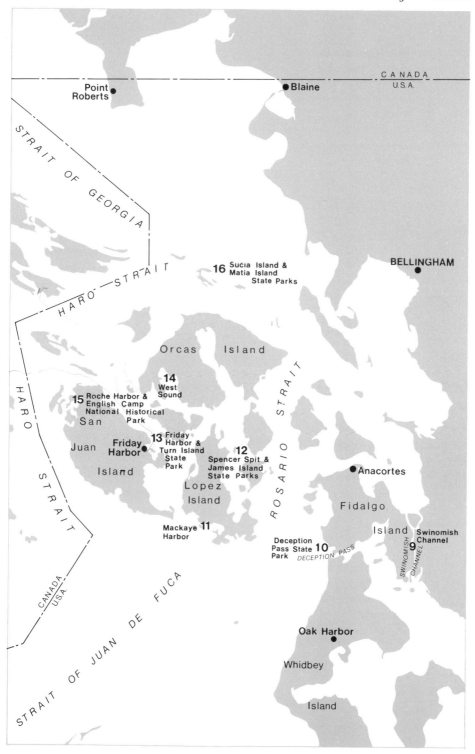

CANADA
U.S.A.

Point
Roberts

● Blaine

BELLINGHAM ●

STRAIT OF GEORGIA

HARO STRAIT

16 Sucia Island &
Matia Island
State Parks

Orcas   Island

14
West
Sound

15 Roche Harbor &
English Camp
National Historical
Park

San

Juan

Friday
Harbor ●

13 Friday
Harbor &
Turn Island
State
Park

12
Spencer Spit &
James Island
State Parks

Island

Lopez
Island

● Anacortes

Fidalgo

Island   Swinomish
Channel

ROSARIO STRAIT

HARO

STRAIT

Mackaye **11**
Harbor

Deception
Pass State **10**
Park *DECEPTION PASS*

SWINOMISH
CHANNEL

9

CANADA
U.S.A.

STRAIT OF JUAN DE FUCA

● Oak Harbor

Whidbey

Island

45

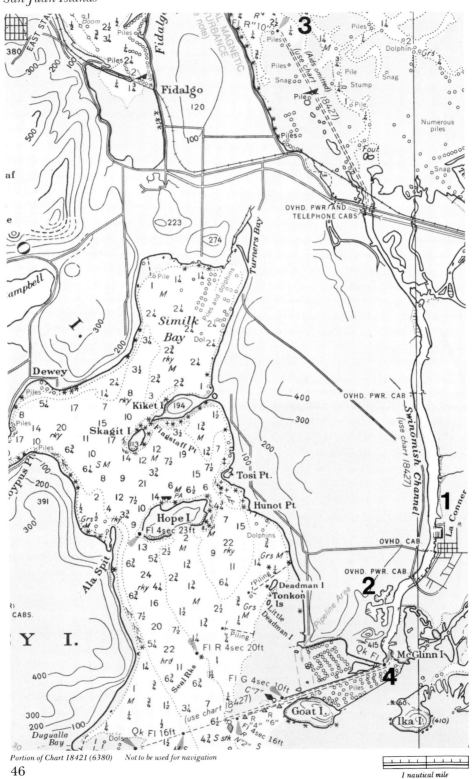

1 nautical mile

9

Swinomish Channel

What's There the calm "inside" route....historical sites and attractions....smelt jigging....freshly smoked salmon....waterfront businesses and cafes....

Charts

18427 (6376) Anacortes to Skagit Bay   1:25,000
18423 (184-SC) small craft chart:
    Bellingham to Everett including San Juan Islands;
    inset of Swinomish Channel   1:40,000

Moorage Visitors' moorage at the large Port of Skagit County Marina at La Conner;[1] temporary moorage at guest docks at La Conner and at Shelter Bay,[2] a privately developed community

Facilities Complete marina and repair services at La Conner, as well as the facilities of a small but tourist-oriented community

Caution Controlling depth in Swinomish Channel is about 2.7 metres (9 feet). The channel can be difficult to navigate in fog or strong wind, and the unlighted buoys are difficult to follow at night.

    Allow for currents when docking and, when tying up, fender well against boat wash damage. Obey speed limits posted.

Bridges entering from Padilla Bay:[3]

    Railway swing bridge clearance, 1.5 metre (5 feet); left open except at the approach of a train

    Highway lift bridge clearance, 4.9 metre (16 feet); signal 4 blasts to open or phone 466-3281. Manned 24 hours

    Note: especially with a following current, keep well clear of a bridge until it is fully opened.

Access By car, along both sides of the channel

    Launching ramps: La Conner; Shelter Bay

There is nothing in all the Pacific Northwest like the trip along the Swinomish Channel to La Conner.

Like a little piece of Europe: this canal passes through farmland drained and dyked, past picnic tables on the banks, and along the lawns of shoreside houses.

Like a small river: ten miles long, if you count the dredged approaches in Padilla Bay and Skagit Bay, with ranges, buoys and pilings marking a way once navigated by sternwheelers and now by tugs with log booms, by fishboats, and by a fleet of pleasure craft. This back-alley route passes Fidalgo Island, a route passable in any weather and not blocked by rapids.

And at La Conner, like a main street: speed limits posted to minimize the wash, and shoreline businesses with parking spaces for boats: pull in for a meal, to stock up on groceries, or to sit in a waterfront tavern.

Except at Hole in the Wall,[4] where the "canal" or "river" shoulders past a steep rock cliff, the Swinomish Channel winds leisurely past mud banks very rich in clams: hundreds of waterspouts stab into the air at low tides. In Padilla Bay, good crabbing. Smelt in the channel during winter months, and in February La Conner hosts the only smelt derby in the world.

La Conner is a living museum. Buy a bag of seed from the oldest operating seed company in the Northwest. Or buy a copy of Washington State's oldest weekly newspaper. Or wander by a hand-tooled log cabin, a landmark mansion being restored, and streets of gingerbread-and-gable houses. The Skagit County Museum gives views of both time and distance: inside, displays of pioneer life; and outside, a wonderful view of the Cascade Mountains, and of the Skagit Flats, continuously farmed for a century. A view almost aerial from this hilltop: the farms giving the museum a distant patchwork quilt of subtle colours.

Within a few blocks of the channel, a modern dry dock and an ancient fire wagon. Dugout canoes and sleek fibreglass fishboats. Salmon being barbecued beside a restaurant. Smoked fish and oysters on the Indian Reserve. The old town centre and the instant community of Shelter Bay. And boat-related businesses of all sorts. A unique area to cruise.

Did you know: When the Rainbow Bridge over the Swinomish Channel was newly painted with metal primer, the people of La Conner liked the colour so much that they decided to leave the bridge bright orange.

Smelt à la Conner

Don't bother scaling smelt. To clean them, simply snip the heads off, with scissors if you like, and cut off the back and belly fins. Slit each fish open along the belly and wash out the viscera. To bone smelt: slip your thumbnail under the backbone and tug it gently up and back toward the tail. All the little bones will come out at once.

1 pound smelt, about a dozen
¼ cup ground cereal (cornmeal, or Vita B, or finely ground corn flakes or cracker crumbs)
salt and pepper to flavour
2 tablespoons finely grated Parmesan cheese

Clean and bone the smelt. Combine the cereal, spices and cheese in a plastic bag. Drop the smelt one by one into the bag and shake it until the fish is well coated. Pan-fry the coated fish in hot fat until both sides are golden brown and crisp.

About 20 minutes to prepare.

Serves 3 to 4

The street of water at La Conner

Under soaring Deception Pass Bridge

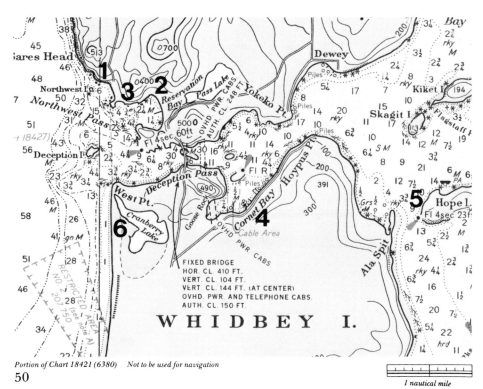

1 nautical mile

10

Deception Pass State Park

What's There 2339 acres of state park....spectacular currents....scuba diving....sandy beaches....deer....easy access to fresh-water lakes....fishing....camping....hiking....developed areas and wilderness....

Charts

18427 (6376) Anacortes to Skagit Bay	1:25,000
18423 (184-SC) small craft chart:	
Bellingham to Everett including San Juan Islands; inset of Deception Pass	1:25,000

Moorage In Rosario Bay[1] and Reservation Bay,[2] good-weather anchorage

In Sharpe Cove,[3] a landing float

In Cornet Bay,[4] state park pier and mooring buoys; berths and private mooring basin

At Hope Island,[5] mooring buoys

Facilities At Cornet Bay, marina facilities, cafe, groceries, laundromat and hot showers, accommodation

Deception Pass State Park: camping and picnic sites, toilets, showers, shelters; a concession stand by Cranberry Lake open during the summer months

At Hope Island, wilderness; no development, and no fires permitted

Caution The currents in Deception Pass may reach 8 knots: to avoid the turbulence and whirlpools, negotiate the pass near time of slack current. Fog and small boats in the opening of the pass often complicate navigation.

Access Car access via bridges over the Swinomish Channel or by car ferry from Mukilteo (near Everett) to southern Whidbey Island; to Hope Island by boat only

Launching ramps: Cornet Bay; Reservation Bay

Deception Pass State Park — a boaters' playground on a grand scale: 2339 acres. An astonishing variety of attractions. Where else could you land at a wave-washed gravel beach, buy a snack, sunbathe on sand, and swim in a lake — all within a few minutes' walk? That's West Beach, separated from Cranberry Lake by only a narrow bridge of gravel and luxurious sand. Easy to carry a dinghy over to the lake. Unique! Campsites nearby, and picnic tables by a concession stand: a perfect place for small-boat camping.

Northwest Pass is for underwater sightseeing, a marine life preserve attracting recreation divers and entire classes of students from the biology outstation at Rosario Beach. Something for all divers here: currents or calm water, deep water or reefs, rock or sand. And lots of shallow water for just snorkelling along.

Reservation Bay features a landing float in Sharpe Cove and many excuses for coming ashore: pretty little Pass Lake a short and shady walk away, for swimming or fly-fishing; or the shoreline trail to Lighthouse Point; or the forest walks under tall timber. Children like the bay for its beach, for the grass fields, for the playground near the shore, and most of all for the sassy squirrels so brave for the sake of handouts.

At few places along the coast is there such variety in one park. And different seasons multiply still more its possibilities.

Deception Pass itself deserves to be taken seriously: deep and clear of rocks but very, very turbulent when running full. Even at slack water the pass makes me feel diminished. Maybe it's the power of immovable rock on either side forcing water to such furious motion. Or maybe it's the bridge arched overhead. I'm always relieved to be through. A curious sensation.

Did you know: In 1792 Master Joseph Whidbey of Captain George Vancouver's exploring party found the narrow pass between the two islands. Captain Vancouver, who had thought Whidbey Island to be a peninsula, named the pass "Deception".

Something to Try: Scuba Diving

Scuba diving is a sport beautifully compatible with boating, another dimension to the adventure of exploring water. And one that depends little on weather. Puget Sound and the Strait of Georgia abound with good diving sites. The underwater reserve near Rosario Beach is a good spot for beginners. Why not take a diving course, and suit up?

If you've ever wanted to stroke a fish, Rosario Beach is the place you can probably do so. The bottom is crawling with red Irish lords. Although I wouldn't say they like back scratching, they tolerate it.

Rosario Beach and the waters around are within Deception Pass State Park, an underwater reserve. You must not take any marine life, however the spot is excellent for sightseeing in a wild setting. This is the unique offering of Rosario. Unlike many of the sites in this area, Rosario is a totally natural scene. No man-made pilings to attract animals. No jetty. Just bottom kelp, bull kelp, red and green seaweed feathering up in the water and the most urchins I've seen anywhere — both green ones and giant red ones. The rocks off Rosario Head are well-named Urchin Rocks.

Many other animals live here, too. Millions of little transparent shrimp hop and skitter about like a field of grasshoppers in July. Big frothy white plumose anemones, kelp greenlings, octopuses, Oregon tritons, gum boot chitons and thousands of spider crabs.

But mostly my impression of Rosario is of a tremendous burst of urchins whose spines quiver and glow, and of sluggish slow red Irish lords that I could hold in my hand.

by Betty Pratt-Johnson
from *141 Dives*

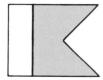

blue and white
International Code of Signals "A", which indicates, "I have a diver down; keep well clear at slow speed."

red and white
Signal flag in general use by divers.

A touch of the past at Mackaye Harbor

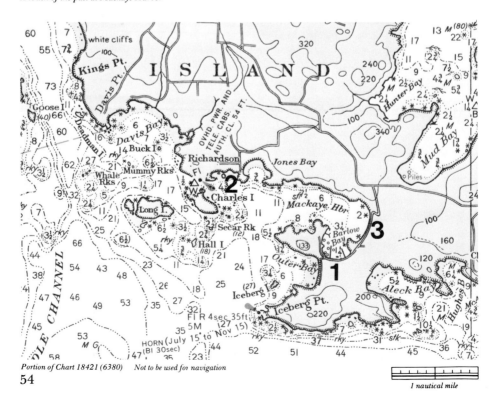

Portion of Chart 18421 (6380)   Not to be used for navigation

1 nautical mile

11

Mackaye Harbor

What's There old-style general store....fresh fish....sandy
beaches....commercial fishing fleet....an interesting inn....hot
cinnamon buns....underwater rocks covered with abalone....

Charts
18423 (184-SC) small craft chart:
    Bellingham to Everett including San Juan Islands;
    inset of Mackaye Harbor   1:25,000
18421 (6380) Strait of Juan de Fuca to Strait of Georgia   1:80,000

Moorage In Barlow Bay,[1] good anchorage, but during the fishing
season anchor well away from the main channels or suffer endless
night-time noise and wash

    The wharves are for cannery boats only

    At Richardson,[2] tie against the pilings of the wharf face

Facilities Near Barlow Bay, a fresh fish outlet; inn with restaurant

    At Richardson Store, groceries, charts, hardware, fresh baking
and fuel

Caution Many shoals and reefs lurk in the area.

Access By car ferry from Anacortes or from Sidney, B.C., to
Upright Head on northern Lopez Island

    Launching ramp: the nearest, an unsurfaced ramp at
Fisherman Bay

The horn at Iceberg Point blows long, low tones. No other part of the San Juan Islands quite gives the exciting sensation of ocean-edge remoteness. The outer open side of the islands takes the brunt of winter storms. The trees lean inland. The rocks are ground down. Even during summer calms the Strait of Juan de Fuca hints of ocean swells, and the kelp beds surge uneasily.

Mackaye Harbor's a fishing outpost, a place of waiting for the open fishing days. Seiners and trollers raft here several deep when not working. Nets stretch along the floats. A derelict hull leans against the shore, bow pointed upward as though still climbing waves. In summer, fishermen and their families make gypsy camps of tents and trailers in the fields around the harbour, to wait out the lay-off days.

The only buildings seen from the harbour are a seafood store, a few farm homes, and the Mackaye Harbor Inn.[3] Beach a boat right in front of the inn. It is a converted house, and still so much a house that one feels like knocking before entering. The dining room set as if for Sunday dinner guests, and an upstairs lounge like a living room, with a window-view of the harbour.

Richardson is a tidal reference point with a long, long history: the first port of call for steamers that shuttled between Puget Sound and the San Juan Islands. The store alone is worth the cruise to Mackaye Harbor. The building is very old, and built out on pilings that straddle a shoreside reef. The wharf obviously built for coastal freighters and fishboats that belly against it comfortably enough. But don't hesitate. Go in. The stop is fun. Tie your boat to the barnacled pilings, and scale a vertical ladder — an operation easiest at high tide. Buy your groceries, place them in the basket at the end of the hand-operated crane, and lower them to your boat.

The store is "general" in the old-fashioned sense, selling everything from hardware to hard tack, and smelling wonderfully of candles and fresh cookies. Choose cinnamon buns and oatmeal bread still too hot to eat, and take some of the scent away with you.

Did you know: An abalone can exert suction up to several thousand times its own weight.

Abalone: Steak-of-the-Sea

An abalone is a meaty muscle housed in a shell as pretty as the meat is good to eat: the shell, an ear-shaped covering lined with lustrous mother-of-pearl; the meat, delicate, irresistible. The filet mignon of seafood: no wonder abalone are more difficult to find each year.

But try it, if only to taste one once. To find abalone of legal size you must usually dive, or at least snorkel during a low tide. Look for abalone on rocky underwater shelves and reefs and ledges, wherever the water is high in salinity and chillingly cold in temperature.

Sneak up on an abalone. The creature's foot clings with a lusty persistence to a rock: the more so when sensing a threat. To capture abalone requires a quick flip of a metal bar. In theory. In practice, more often a rugged tug-of-war and vigorous prying.

Shuck an abalone by working a knife between the meat and shell, or try the easy way: drop the entire creature into boiling water. When the muscle relaxes, you can more easily free the edible foot from its shell. Cut off the stomach, being careful not to break the sac. Wash the meat in cold running water, and slice across the grain into slabs about half an inch thick. The steaks must be tenderized, pounded with a mallet or hammer until they are limp.

> Dip each steak in beaten egg.
> Dredge in seasoned flour.
> Sauté. Perhaps in butter to which a chopped clove of garlic has been added.
> Cook for only one minute on each side.
> Serve hot. With a squeeze of lemon.

abalone

Picnic site at James Island State Park

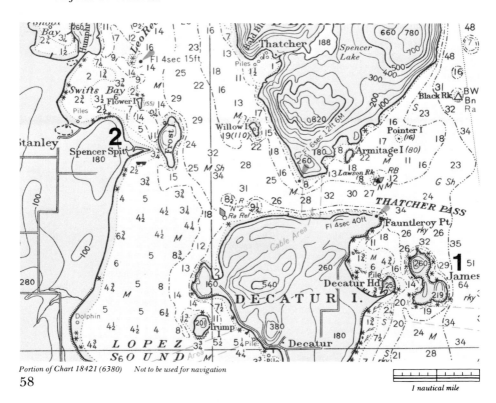

Portion of Chart 18421 (6380)   Not to be used for navigation

1 nautical mile

12

Spencer Spit State Park and James Island State Park

What's There pebble beaches....camping and picnic sites....wild rabbits....good fishing....ranger on duty....beachcombing....snorkelling....small-boat camping....

Charts
18423 (184-SC) small craft chart:
    Bellingham to Everett including San Juan Islands   1:80,000
18421 (6380) Strait of Juan de Fuca to Strait of Georgia   1:80,000

Moorage James Island:[1] a small landing dock and several mooring buoys; anchorage on the west side is open to tidal eddies
    Spencer Spit:[2] mooring buoys and anchorage

Facilities James Island State Park: 114 acres, campsites, pit toilets, trails; no drinking water
    Spencer Spit State Park, accessible to car traffic and heavily used during the summer: 130 acres, campsites, pit toilets, shelter, picnic tables, water, ranger residence

Caution The currents around James Island can be difficult to row against: keep a close watch on children playing in dinghies.

Access Car access to Spencer Spit State Park via ferries from Anacortes or from Sidney, B.C., to Upright Head on Lopez Island
    By boat only to James Island
    Launching ramps: nearby, at Peavine Pass, Blakely Island; several on Orcas Island

Spencer Spit grows inch by sand-and-gravel inch toward Frost Island. Boats can still pass easily around the end of the spit, but a depth sounder indicates that the gap is becoming more and more shallow.

Driftwood, and some incredibly large drift trees, are heaped along the spit, with a tangle of tide wrack, shells and sand dollars. Hours of beachcombing. Alive, the sand dollars are a sooty black; dead, they are pale and fragile. Find them, but please leave them for someone else to see. Removing sea life, except for the edible species regulated by the State Department of Fisheries, is unlawful in state parks. Be aware of riparian rights on neighbouring beaches — the courts regularly levy fines on people who invade the clam beds.

A fascinating salt-water lagoon has formed within the sandspit. High tide refills and refreshens the pool; low tide landlocks it. A showplace for a great variety of swimming, creeping and flying creatures. A good place for bug watching, for bird watching, and, when summer tourists come, for people watching.

Rabbits! At dusk the entire hillside above the park twitches with rabbits. Big rabbits and small rabbits, shy ones and bold ones, in solid colours and in patches. Dozens of them hop and nibble on the lawn under the flagpole of the park: a fantasy of rabbits cavorting in the moonlight.

James Island, a little over three miles away, a very different sort of park. Maybe because it's out in Rosario Strait, the island seems so clean and fresh: the winds and the currents keep scrubbing it.

A knobby bone of an island, almost chewed through at the middle. Barely 100 metres between the west bay and the east. The narrow neck manages to be a ridge and a valley and a parkland of pine, all at once, with a thick underfooting of soft pine needles. The landing dock is on the west side, but morning sunshine and the other beach is only a few minutes away.

Explore James Island leisurely, bit by bit. Hiking trails criss-cross the island. Wild rabbits at almost every turn of the trail. Or the same rabbit, hopping ahead of us? Climb the eighty-metre peak on the north side for a smug king-of-the-castle feeling and a wonderful view.

Wade in the tidepools or drift in a dinghy over the reefs by the shore to see the brilliantly coloured anemones. Stare down into the deep water at the edge of a shoreline drop-off. Hypnotizing. Down...down...and still seeing starfish clinging to the rocks.

Did you know: There is no poison oak on the San Juan Islands.

State Marine Parks in the San Juan Islands

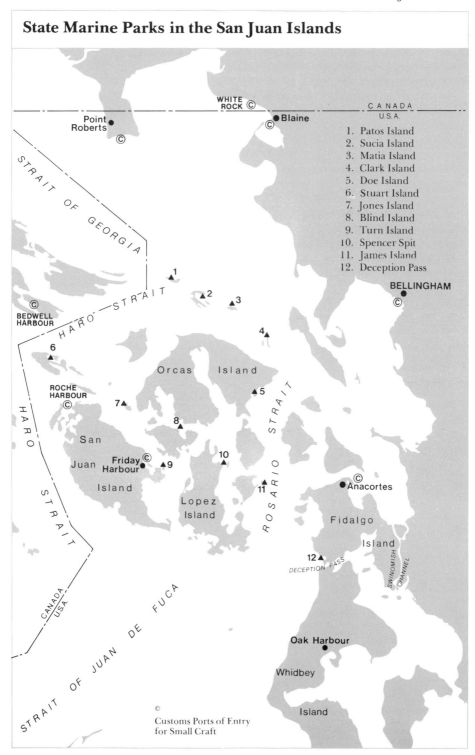

1. Patos Island
2. Sucia Island
3. Matia Island
4. Clark Island
5. Doe Island
6. Stuart Island
7. Jones Island
8. Blind Island
9. Turn Island
10. Spencer Spit
11. James Island
12. Deception Pass

© Customs Ports of Entry for Small Craft

Friday Harbor Laboratories

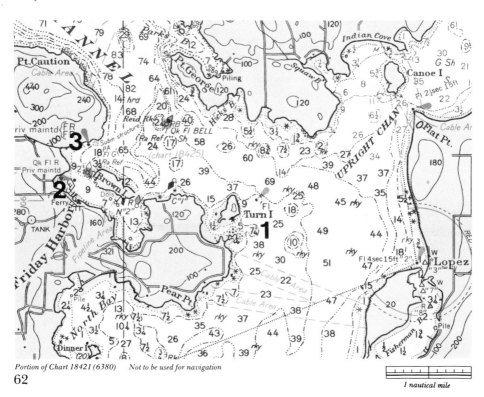

Portion of Chart 18421 (6380)   Not to be used for navigation

1 nautical mile

13

Friday Harbor and Turn Island State Park

What's There unique tour of an oceanographic institute....Port of Entry....shopping....historic sites....deer and wild rabbits within town limits....an island state park....scuba diving in clear, clear water....

Charts

18425 (6379) San Juan Channel   1:20,000
18423 (184-SC) small craft chart:
     Bellingham to Everett including San Juan Islands;
     inset of Friday Harbor   1:20,000

Moorage At Turn Island State Park,[1] mooring buoys
   In Friday Harbour,[2] mooring floats at marinas and at the port wharf

Facilities Complete boating and tourist supplies and facilities, including an inter-island medical clinic, at Friday Harbor
   Hot showers in the Customs building
   Turn Island State Park: 35 acres, campsites, tables, trails, pit toilets; no drinking water

Caution The currents in Friday Harbor can make docking difficult. Keep clear of ferry traffic.

Access By car ferry from Anacortes or from Sidney, B.C., to Friday Harbor
   Boat access only to Turn Island
   Launching ramp: Friday Harbor

Friday Harbor is a *must*. Bustling, busy, often crowded. The main place of business, the county seat, a Port of Entry, and the only incorporated village in the San Juan Islands. Post a letter, do your laundry, see a film, or balance a propeller. Or just look around. It's a nice town for that too, with lots of little shops to browse in, old buildings, historic sites, and a museum.

Best of all, visit the University of Washington Oceanographic Laboratory.[3] Some facilities open to public view; guided tours of fascinating displays and experiments. Salt-water tanks with creatures not usually seen so near, if seen at all: a garden of anemones, starfish in rainbow colours, a pulsing cloud of jellyfish, sea urchins like underwater porcupines, and a bush-like basket star. A dogfish, swimming in a large round tank, stood on its tail, head out of the water, the better to look back at us. We patted it, with ginger regard for the shark's teeth. It wriggled like a puppy: it liked the attention! The guide showed how sand dollars tip themselves on edge to lean against the current that brings them food. How flounders flutter down into the sand to hide — one eye up in order to keep watch. How a scallop escapes a starfish by using jet propulsion to squirt away.

On the grounds wild rabbits by the dozens fed on immaculate lawns and well-tended shrubbery, and a doe and her tiny fawn delicately picked their way along the shore.

Turn Island State Park is good for small-boat camping: all the sensations of being in wilderness, but conveniently close to supplies and civilization. For any boater, a refreshing stop, a quiet place to stay awhile.

Strong currents swirl around the island, but because of the wealth of current-loving underwater life and the clear, clean water, this spot is popular with divers. Handy to have campsites so near a good diving area.

Surprising to see deer on such a small island, but there they stood, sun-flecked hides almost invisible among the arbutus trees. On the gravel beach, teredo-eaten wood chips, as fragile as the finest lace.

Did you know: The Pacific Northwest octopus is the largest in the world, some of these shy creatures having an armspread of six metres (twenty feet).

Customs Ports of Entry: Puget Sound and San Juan Islands

Call your intended Port of Entry to ask their business hours: pleasure vessels wishing to clear customs at other than regular times must pay a fee. For more customs information, and the phone numbers of southern British Columbia Ports of Entry, see page 83.

Anacortes	(206) 293-2331	see map, page 63
Bellingham	(206) 734-5460	see map, page 63
Blaine	(206) 332-5771	see map, page 63, 135
Everett	(206) 259-0246	see map, page 25
Friday Harbor	(206) 378-2080	see map, page 63, 97
Neah Bay	(206) 645-2312	Strait of Juan de Fuca
Olympia (phone Tacoma)	(206) 593-6336	see map, page 25
Port Angeles	(206) 457-4311	Strait of Juan de Fuca
Port Townsend	(206) 385-3777	see map, page 25
Roche Harbor	(206) 378-4169	see map, page 63, 97
Seattle	(206) 442-5491	see map, page 25
Tacoma	(206) 593-6336	see map, page 25

A customs clearing station is planned for Point Roberts Marina. Phone Point Roberts Customs (206) 945-2314 for further information.

Customs dock

Dinner and a driftwood fire

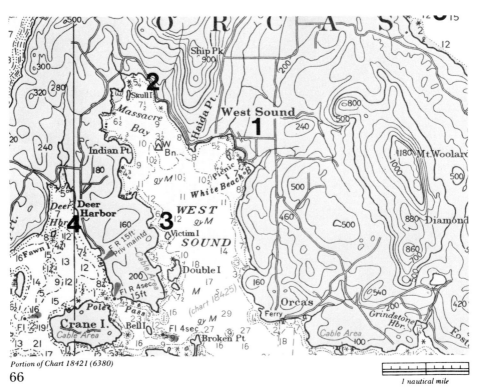

Portion of Chart 18421 (6380)

1 nautical mile

14

West Sound

What's There miniature island parks....country walks....wild
flowers....old general store....shoreside totem
pole....shrimps....crabs....

Charts
18425 (6379) San Juan Channel   1:20,000
18423 (184-SC) small craft chart:
       Bellingham to Everett including San Juan Islands;
       inset of Roche Harbor   1:40,000

Moorage Moorage slips at the marina and temporary visitors'
moorage at the yacht club float; good anchorage

Facilities At West Sound[1] community, marina services and a
general store with book-trade shelves
    Skull Island[2] and Victim Island[3] are undeveloped state park
islands; no drinking water

Caution A brisk south wind can funnel up the Sound: keep that in
mind when choosing an anchorage.
    Approaching West Sound from the west, beware the "rock pile"
in the channel.

Access By car ferry from Anacortes or from Sidney, B.C., to
Orcas Island
    Launching ramps: nearby, at Deer Harbor[4] and at East Sound[5]

Deer Harbor, on one side, draws boaters by the dozens; and East Sound, on the other side, needs no advertising; but West Sound, in the middle, is generally overlooked.

The place names might be discouraging. Skull Island. Victim Island. Massacre Bay. Grisly names, but a beautiful setting. Ideal places for ghost stories around evening campfires. Ideal islands for small-boat camping: well away from heavy traffic, but with supplies within easy reach. Water you must bring with you. The islands are small, but still islands, with all the essentials of an island in miniature. Beaches five metres long. Anchorage for one boat at a time. Some grass, and moss, and shade, and sunny ledges. All just right for a lazy afternoon picnic. Choose an island — you'll probably have it to yourself.

Excellent crabbing in West Sound. A large Dungeness without even trying: he just climbed onto a lure let down to bottom-fish. The crab net brought in more crabs and an enormous sun star as well.

West Sound, the only village here, has a well-equipped marina and a very pleasant general store. Pleasant walking, hereabouts: masses of peas, golden poppies, and blue-purple chicory grow wild and colourful along the road. Enough turns and bends along the way to lead you on, just one corner more. Better take a snack: you may go miles before you want to turn around.

Did you know: Many place names in West Sound — Skull Island, Victim Island, Massacre Bay, Haida Point, Indian Point — refer to a history of war and carnage between slave-hunting Haidas from the north and the resident Lummi Indians.

Wild flowers on West Sound

Roche Harbor: history, luxury, and masses of flowers

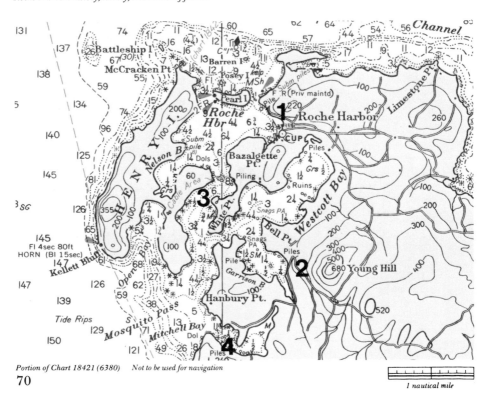

Portion of Chart 18421 (6380)   Not to be used for navigation

1 nautical mile

15

Roche Harbor and English Camp National Historical Park

What's There a strange mausoleum....horseback riding....ruins of lime works and quarries....waterfront dining....Port of Entry....historical sites....archaeological "digs"....interpretive centre with slide shows, talks....

Charts

18425 (6379) San Juan Channel	1:20,000
18423 (184-SC) small craft chart:	
Bellingham to Everett including San Juan Islands;	
inset of Roche Harbor	1:40,000

Moorage At Roche Harbor,[1] moorage slips for guests near the resort, excellent anchorage

In Garrison Bay near English Camp National Historical Park,[2] anchorage; currents may cause anchors to drag

Facilities At Roche Harbor, complete resort facilities: hotel and cabins, tennis courts and swimming pool; groceries and souvenirs, restaurant, shower and laundry facilities; marina services including boat rentals and charters

English Camp National Park: trails, toilets, interpretive centre; no drinking water

No fires permitted

Caution Negotiate Mosquito Pass[3] with care: it winds around several shoal patches.

Access Car access to both Roche Harbor and English Camp; car ferries to San Juan Island from Anacortes and from Sidney, Vancouver Island

Landing field near Roche Harbor

Launching ramps: Roche Harbor; Mitchell Bay[4]

A company town, and now a tourist resort: in Roche Harbor the layers of the past blend with the life of the present. A brick-paved roadway and an airstrip. An old log cabin and an Olympic-size pool. A hillside of crumbling masonry and machinery, and a harbour full of pleasure boats. The shoreline a delight for photographers: white church, magnificent old hotel, and masses of flowers against a background of dark trees.

John S. McMillin built the Hotel de Haro in 1886 for dignitaries visiting his company town. The lobby-library as dark and mellow as aged leather, and old pictures of the community hanging on the walls. Teddy Roosevelt signed the guest book, but the page on which he signed was stolen in 1977.

Signs point the way to the McMillin Mausoleum but the route is confusing — some signs must be missing. Walk toward the airstrip, turn left and follow the hillside road up past a graveyard until you see the sign pointing out the trail to the right. Or cross the playing field, pass the pool and tennis courts, and follow the riding trail up the hill.

The mausoleum, "Afterglow", is a strange, still place: a theatre of shapes and shadows. Pillars and fluted columns and chair-shaped crypts around a stone table. Rows of benches on one side add to the effect of high drama, and only wait for the actors.

English Camp, or more properly "British Camp", is a shrine of a different sort. A memorial to the "Pig War", the site of the British garrison during the twelve years' stand-off over the ownership of the San Juans. Trails, a few rotted pilings, orchard trees, split-rail fences and grassy acres of parade ground sketch out some details of military life a century ago. Bits of the original blockhouse and barracks and commissary still stand; the rest, imagined. The park is the site of active archaeological "digs": the interpretive centre displays the shards of pottery, arrow heads and other "finds". The stylized garden adds a strange touch of formality.

Did you know: The gun that shot the pig hangs over the tourist curios in the grocery store at Roche Harbor.

The War that Wasn't

June 15, 1859, by shooting a British pig, an American, Lyman Cutler, brought to a boil a long-simmering border dispute. The 49th parallel stood as the boundary between British and American land and though the British had claims on Vancouver Island the rest of the border was left dangling somewhere in the Strait of Georgia. The British opted for Rosario Strait as the boundary line; the Americans for Haro Strait. In between lay the San Juan Islands.

Step by step, events replaced decisions. The Hudson's Bay Company sent sheep to graze on San Juan Island and the Americans tried to collect taxes on the sheep. The British sent more livestock to the island, and the Americans sent surveyors to stake the land. Settlers from both sides moved in. Both sides sent magistrates to keep the law. And then a British pig developed an appetite for American potatoes, and died in the act of international trespass. Military forces moved in, and feelings escalated. Within a few months American soldiers had formed an armed camp at the south of the island, and the British, in armed ships, were standing by.

Yet now a series of careful, calm decisions doused the spark that might have exploded into war. Both sides agreed to joint occupancy of the island until the boundary could be settled: the English set up camp at Garrison Bay, the Americans at Griffin Bay. They remained so for twelve more years, until the dispute was referred to the Emperor of Germany who decided that the border should follow Haro Strait, and the San Juan Islands be American. In 1872 the British left the island. The pig had been the only casualty of the long occupation.

English Camp on Garrison Bay

A calm-weather anchorage at Matia Island

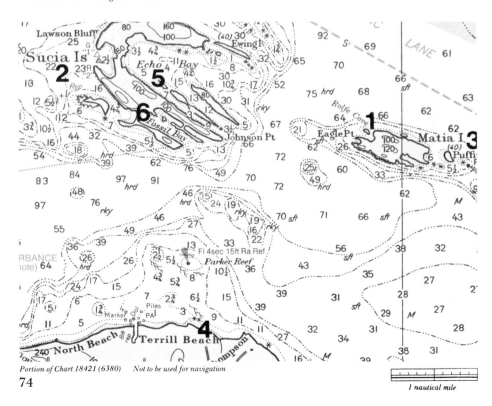

Portion of Chart 18421 (6380)   Not to be used for navigation

1 nautical mile

16

Sucia Island State Park And Matia Island State Park

What's There interesting rock formations....cormorants and puffins and seals....scuba diving and snorkelling....beachcombing....walking trails....small-boat camping....fossils....

Charts
18423 (184-SC) small craft chart:
Bellingham to Everett including San Juan Islands 1:80,000
18421 (6380) Strait of Juan de Fuca to the Strait of
Georgia   1:80,000

Moorage Matia Island:[1] mooring buoys and a landing dock
Sucia Island:[2] mooring buoys, landing docks, and several good anchorages

Facilities Matia Island: 145 acres, water, campsites, pit toilets
Sucia Island, most developed of the chain of park islands: 562 acres, campsites, shelters, pit toilets, water, trails, information bulletin boards, state parks' personnel in attendance

Caution Many rocks and reefs hide in the waters surrounding these islands: allow for currents which may set you closer to shallow water than you intend.

Access By boat only
Launching ramp : nearby, at Terrill Beach,[4] Orcas Island

Matia Island is wildlife preserve, state marine park, an island with endlessly fascinating rockscapes along the shore. Curves and caves and pillars of rock; stone froth and honeycombs, and stony icing swirls.

Matia is Spanish for "no protection" but during reasonable summer weather the anchorages are comfortable enough. Drinking water on the northwest side of the island, but you must work for it. Pleasant work: from the wharf, follow a forest trail to a clearing around a hand-operated pump. Worth the walk on a hot day just to feel this damp cedar shade.

Take a close look but do not land at Puffin Island,[3] a bird sanctuary. A glorious piece of rock, all fluid shapes and colour-layered swirls of stone. Ledges underline the ragged black rows of cormorants, and hide the showy puffins that give the island its name. Below, on a tidal rock, a herd of sunning seals: the little ones roll and tumble among the drowsing parents. But watch through binoculars: bring your boat too near, and within seconds every seal disappears.

Sucia is the best known, the most developed, and by far the largest of the San Juan Island state marine parks. Sucia means "foul" or "dirty" and refers to the many rocks and reefs and shoals that complicate navigation near the island but that attract fishermen and scuba divers with the richness of the marine life near such shallows. Shiners swarm around the park wharf pilings: fair game for children.

An information bulletin board near Fossil Bay shows the layout of the park and tells of the sporadic farming that left the cisterns and chimney stones, and the traces of fields and fences and fruit trees; tells of the logging that left the rough roads now so pleasant to follow; and of the sandstone quarry that once brought a thousand workers to live on the island.

Sucia Island is used now as public parkland because of the efforts of E.V. Henry who spearheaded a move to buy up the land and place it in trust for public use. A plaque honours this man and honours the dozens of Puget Sound yacht clubs that saw this massive project through. Fittingly, the southernmost spot of Sucia Island has been named E.V. Henry Point.

Gunkhole the boomerang curve of Echo Bay:[5] you could come here often, each time selecting a different beach, another walk, a change of anchorage. And fossils in Fossil Bay?[6] Of course! Look along the sandstone bluff across from the floats: the stone here is friable, not far changed from sand, and the fossils stand out in layers of white fragments and as complete and perfect shells. Such delicate things to be preserved so long!

Did you know: The little bays of Sucia Island were once hideaways for smugglers carrying Chinese labourers, opium, wool, and liquor between the United States and Canada.

76

Something to Try: Catching "Shiners"

Any child will tell you that catching a bucket full of shiners is more fun per pound than catching a single salmon, and children are real judges of such matters. Shiners, or shiner seaperch, are plentiful in any season. They are easy to catch with cheap and simple gear that will keep a child busy for hours at any wharf:

— the smallest hooks you can find, size 12 or 14
— shot weights, or old bolts, or any piece of metal to weigh down the line
— thin fishing line, or even thread
— bait: pieces of mussel, or seaworm, or tiny crabs
— a bucket of seawater in which to keep the fish alive

Shiner fishing is a very practical business: none of this throwing hooks into "empty" water! The fish hunt in schools along the pilings. You can see them. No use fishing if you don't. Lower a baited hook and gently jig the line. Shiners feed enthusiastically, and the same fish, thrown back, takes the hook again and again. The littlest fish are often the bravest: they dart in first and cannily take the bait without the hook. The fun is to watch them at it.

Throw the fish back if you don't intend to use it, or keep it alive in a bucket of seawater set in a shady place, but change the water often to keep it cool and full of oxygen. Shiners are quite edible, though bony: try them cleaned and scaled, coated with seasoned flour or cornmeal, and fried in butter or bacon fat until they are crisp and nicely browned. Or parlay a small fish into a larger one: use a shiner as bait to catch a cod or rockfish.

Chapter Three
Gulf Islands

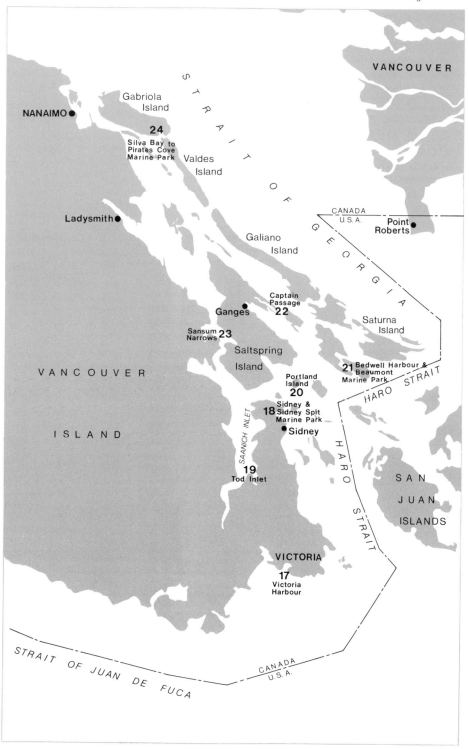

VANCOUVER

Gabriola
Island

NANAIMO ●

24
Silva Bay to
Pirates Cove
Marine Park

Valdes
Island

Ladysmith ●

Galiano
Island

STRAIT OF GEORGIA

CANADA
U.S.A.

Point
Roberts ●

Captain
Passage
22

Ganges ●

Sansum **23**
Narrows

Saltspring

Island

Saturna
Island

21 Bedwell Harbour &
Beaumont
Marine Park

HARO STRAIT

VANCOUVER

Portland
Island
20

Sidney &
18 Sidney Spit
Marine Park
● Sidney

ISLAND

SAANICH INLET

19
Tod Inlet

HARO STRAIT

SAN

JUAN

ISLANDS

VICTORIA

17
Victoria
Harbour

STRAIT OF JUAN DE FUCA

CANADA
U.S.A.

Victoria's Inner Harbour

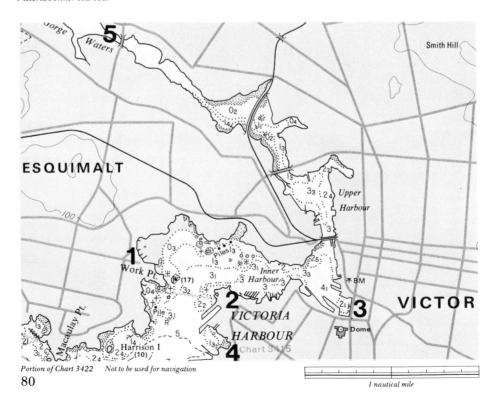

Portion of Chart 3422   Not to be used for navigation

1 nautical mile

17

Victoria Harbour

What's There parks and flowers....shopping....waterways accessible to small boats....large sheltered harbour....Port of Entry....tourist bureau near the moorage area....Parliament Buildings, Empress Hotel, Maritime Museum, Provincial Museum and Archives....

Charts

3415 Victoria Harbour	1:6100
3422 Race Rocks to Discovery Island	1:40,000
3310 small craft charts of Gulf Islands with inset of Victoria Harbour	1:12,000

Moorage In West Bay,[1] marina moorings

At the Fishermens Floats[2] when the fishing fleet is out in summer

In James Bay,[3] mooring slips and buoys in front of the Empress Hotel

Facilities Complete boating and tourist services and supplies

Caution In the harbour, watch for seaplanes, ferries, log booms, and barges.

Bridges entering from the Inner Harbour:

Johnson Street Bridge, clearance 5.8 metres (19 feet); manned 0900 to 2400 except during rush hour on week days, and 0900 to 1600 on weekends and holidays

Point Ellice Bridge, 8.8 metres (29 feet); fixed span

Railway bridge, 1.8 metres (6 feet); usually left open from 1400 until 0730; phone 382-3179 the day before to request an opening during other hours

Access By car or boat

Launching ramps: James Bay Anglers Association ramp[4] near Ogden Point; West Bay Marina[1]

Victoria in summer is beautiful, but Victoria at Christmas time is dazzling. Anchor in the reflected lights of the Parliament Buildings[3] and of the giant Christmas tree. Wet, dirty and cold, and having nothing to lose, ask permission to bath at the Empress. Take a room for the afternoon. Glory for hours in hot water to the eyebrows, in a tub marvellously deep. In summer you can shower at a gas float near the Fishermens Floats, but a bath at the Empress: that's atmosphere! The carillon peals off time with notes that seem to float on water, and at night the carollers sing out over the moorage. And there's nothing more Christmassy than the smell of mince in the Empress lobby at tea time.

The tourist bureau, Undersea Gardens, the Parliament Buildings, Provincial Museum and Provincial Archives, the Maritime Museum — all within sight of the waterfront — warm, dry, endlessly interesting, and many of them free. What better places to spend a chilly winter day? Pick up some of the museum's Natural History Series booklets: compact, pocket-size reference books covering topics from seashore birds to mushrooms.

The Inner and Upper Harbours provide miles of waterfront exploring, all in perfectly protected water. A good project to tackle in a small boat when the Strait of Juan de Fuca is inhospitable. Look over ferries and seaplanes and cruising yachts from foreign oceans. In a small boat at high tide, work your way along the shore and under the bridges of the Upper Harbour, past mills and shipyards, by wharves and warehouses and waterside parks. Visit historic Point Ellice House and, if the tide is high enough, clear Reversing Falls[5] in The Gorge to reach Craigflower Manor, another free museum. Working a boat against the current is a good introduction to historic sites! Victoria trades heavily on its reputation as a "bit of Olde England" even though it is more truly a bit of Old San Francisco, but who would want to argue against double-decker-bus tours and alley shops? Or fish-and-chips and cobbled streets?

Winters are gentle with Victoria. A bit cloudy, perhaps, but what does that matter when violets grow harbour-side in December? In summer, Victoria boasts some of the driest weather in Canada; count on finding more sunshine and flowers here than you're bound to find in any other city on the northwest coast.

Did you know: English skylarks were introduced to the Victoria area in the early 1900s by colonists homesick for the exhilarating skylark songs.

"Going Foreign": Border Crossing between Washington and British Columbia

The business of border crossing is made as quick and easy as possible for pleasure boaters, but certain regulations must be followed to avoid difficulties and delays and a whopper of a fine.

1. Report immediately and directly to the nearest customs office after crossing the International Boundary if you intend to "touch": to anchor, to come alongside a dock, or to contact a hovering vessel. Boaters who, in the course of fishing or cruising, cross and re-cross the border without "touching" need not report.

2. Only the Master of the visiting vessel is permitted to go ashore to locate a customs officer and report the landing. All other persons on the vessel must stay aboard until inspection has been made and clearance given.

3. Have with you the necessary documents:
   — boat registration
   — personal identification, showing citizenship
   — certificate of naturalization, if applicable
   — for persons under 18 years of age not accompanied by an adult, written permission from a parent or guardian to cross the border
   — for persons who are not American or Canadian citizens, the papers required to enter, or return to, either country

4. Know ahead of time exactly what you are allowed to bring into and take out of each country. For helpful information and booklets, write

   Port Director
   U.S. Customs Service
   P.O. Box 280
   Blaine, WA 98230

   Canada Customs
   1001 West Pender Street
   Vancouver, B.C. V6E 2M8

Customs Ports of Entry in Southern British Columbia

Bedwell Harbour	(604) 629-3363	see map, page 63, 97
Campbell River	(604) 287-3761	see map, page 207
Courtenay (Comox)	(604) 334-3424	see map, page 169
Nanaimo	(604) 753-4181	see map, page 97, 169
Powell River (Westview)	(604) 485-2243	see map, page 169, 207
Sidney	(604) 656-2112	see map, page 97
Vancouver	(604) 666-1272/3/4	see map, page 97, 135
Victoria	(604) 388-3339	see map, page 97
White Rock	(604) 531-7581	see map, page 63, 135

For phone numbers of Ports of Entry in Puget Sound and the San Juan Islands, see page 65.

Public wharf at Sidney, and Sidney Island in background

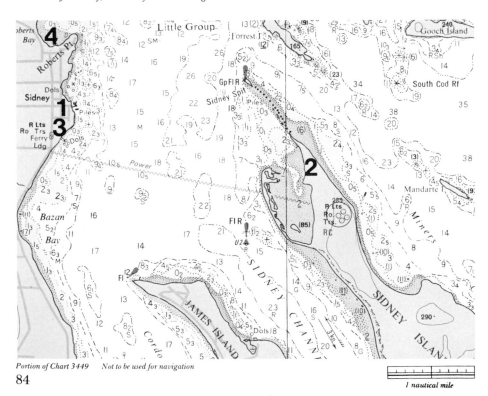

Portion of Chart 3449   Not to be used for navigation

1 nautical mile

18

Sidney, and Sidney Spit Marine Park

What's There Port of Entry....museum....shopping....seafood retail and wholesale store on the public wharf....marine park....excellent small-boat camping....crabbing....

Charts

3451 Discovery Island to Saltspring Island	1:38,000
3310 small craft chart of Gulf Islands	1:40,000

Moorage At Sidney,[1] floats south of the public wharf are exposed to wind, waves and currents, and are removed during the winter; public floats north of the wharf protected by a breakwater

At Sidney Spit Marine Park,[2] enclosing the northern part of Sidney Island, mooring buoys, landing floats, and good anchorage

Facilities At Sidney, laundromat, accommodation, medical services, and various retail outlets including liquor, grocery and hardware stores; marina facilities at Tsehum Harbour, 2 miles north

At Sidney Spit Marine Park, camp and picnic sites, pit toilets, drinking water

Caution Use care when approaching the public floats at Sidney: currents and winds make landing difficult.

Access To Sidney Spit Marine Park by boat only; car access to the city of Sidney; Washington State Ferry Terminal with service to Anacortes and the San Juan Islands

Launching ramps: Bazan Bay;[3] Roberts Bay[4]

Sidney, and Sidney Spit on nearby Sidney Island: together a memorable weekend cruise. The town, for browsing and buying, and for the business of going through customs if coming from the San Juan Islands; the Spit, for good anchorage and for a remarkable explorable parkland.

At Sidney stop for crumpets and for Earl Grey tea. A pleasant town. And a plus for boaters: easy walking; cruising commodities near the wharf; and a grocery store selling gallon cans of maple syrup — a touch of Canadiana, and a delicious souvenir. History in the Sidney municipal museum. Look closely at the collections of antique bottles and Indian artifacts, two things to watch for when cruising.

Sidney Spit, an extravagant stretch of driftwood, pebbles and sand that seems to go on forever, is less than three miles away. Much of the spit would be hidden at high tides, except for the pilings and logs with which the Parks Branch is trying to stabilize the sand and gravel. Shallow water, quickly warmed and safe for swimming. A shady road under big trees connects the park wharf with an older wharf which was once a part of the anchorage now almost entirely silted in. The mooring cleat on the old float could hold a freighter, but the water is barely deep enough to float a canoe.

Nearby, forest gives way to open fields and fences and the ruins of an old brickworks. Rectangular excavations, like small reservoirs, where the brick clay was once dug. Stacks of crumbled bricks, almost hidden by blackberry bushes that yield fruit exceptionally sweet and juicy. And an old brick wall with arched window spaces that frame views of a dozen grazing deer.

Did you know: Sand dabs usually have their eyes on their left side; soles have theirs on the right side; starry flounders may have theirs on either side, but not, unless very young, on both sides.

Camping beside sandy beaches at Sidney Spit Marine Park

Sunken Gardens, Butchart Gardens

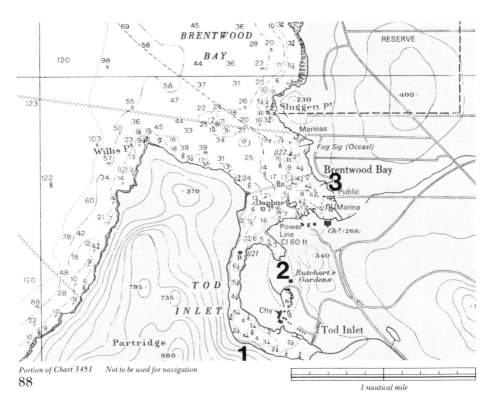

I nautical mile

19

Tod Inlet

What's There a miniature fiord....good clam digging....sheltered anchorage....excellent fishing in Saanich Inlet....Butchart Gardens....

Charts
3310 small craft chart of Gulf Islands   1:40,000
3451 Discovery Island to Saltspring Island   1:38,000

Moorage Anchorage in Tod Inlet[1]
    Mooring buoys and landing float for visitors to Butchart Gardens; no overnight moorage permitted at these floats

Facilities None within the inlet
    At nearby Brentwood Bay,[3] marina services and supplies, and complete sport-fishing facilities, including custom smoking and canning; waterfront dining and various retail stores

Caution Enter Tod Inlet keeping the black spar buoy to your left. The buoy marks a rock at the end of a gravel spit.

Access By boat only, to Tod Inlet; car access to Butchart Gardens
    Launching ramp : nearby, at Brentwood Bay

Tod Inlet, a fantasy world at dusk. The tall chimney of the old lime kiln looming ghostly white in moonlight, like an exotic obelisk over the anchorage. A dark wall of evergreens shuts out the world beyond the inlet. The raucous night-time settling of herons making a strange counterpoint for the concert music coming from the Gardens, a music distant and cedar-strained, almost unreal. And Indians in dugout canoes slipping quietly through the inlet. They were real, and practising for races later in the season.

Daylight shows Tod Inlet differently. Clam beds with enormous butter clams. Water warmed for summer swimming. Water-skiing, dinghy sailing, canoeing, clam digging and fishing, and a large ketch coming in under full sail. Memorable subjects for memorable photographs.

As a special boaters' approach to Butchart Gardens, there are visitors' moorings in a niche at the mouth of Tod Inlet. Tie up here, walk through a gate where the rates are posted, follow a forest trail, and enter at the Japanese garden.

The garden walks are spectacular at any time of the year. In winter the entry rates are very low, yet amazing numbers of flowers still bloom in the mild Saanich Peninsula climate. Even roses in late November.

On summer days the Italian gardens, the rose bowers, the sunken pools, the blaze of colours against the limestone walls and green grass carpeting. On summer nights flower beds coloured by light and floodlit towers of water, reflecting pools and dramatic shadows, and concerts on the lawn. Garden scents and concert sounds drift back to the moorage: the shoreline firs and ferns and cedars seem then to be extensions of the garden display, and all of Tod Inlet seems planned by landscape artists.

Did you know: The thirty-five-acre Butchart Gardens were started in 1904 as an attempt to beautify the deserted limestone quarry once worked for the Butchart family's cement company.

Something to Try: Cruise Photography

According to the kind of logic that works on boats, a camera will never be at hand when you want it. Or you will run out of film when miles up a remote inlet. You will leave the lens cap on during exciting shots. Someone will sit on the camera. Or drop it overboard. Get around the gremlins that follow cameras onto boats:

1. Take more film than you think you will need.
2. Take more pictures than you think you will want.
3. Store all film, new or used, in a cool dark place and develop exposed film as soon as possible.
4. Don't leave a camera in direct sunlight because black cases absorb unexpected amounts of heat even when the air feels cool.
5. Prevent flare-back from reflected light over water by using a lens hood.
6. Protect the lens from scratches and salt spray with a neutral or skylight filter: easy to clean and cheaper than a damaged lens to replace.
7. Try, in a rocking boat, to keep the horizon in your picture horizontal.
8. To gain those sparkling highlights on the water shoot toward, though not right into, the sun.
9. Overexposure is a common problem: count on more light than there seems to be over water.
10. To counter boat movement and engine vibration use a shutter speed of at least 1/250, or use a "fast" film.

And if the camera *does* fall overboard? If you insist on trying to salvage a camera soaked in salt water, do not let the camera dry, and do not take it apart: place it in a pail of fresh water and rush it to a camera specialist.

"Floss", a gravestone in the grass on Portland Island

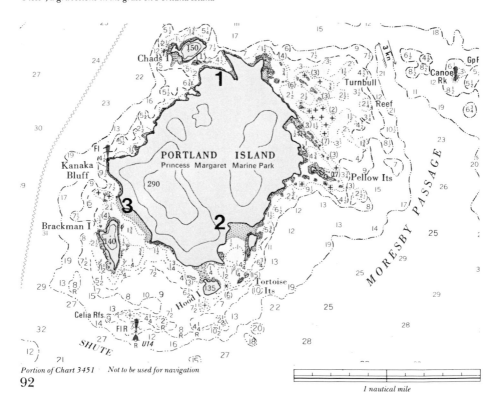

1 nautical mile

20

Portland Island (Princess Margaret Marine Park)

What's There an undeveloped marine park island....abandoned farm buildings and fields....sand beaches....trails....sheep and deer....

Charts
3451 Discovery Island to Saltspring Island   1:38,100
3310 small craft chart of Gulf Island   1:40,000

Moorage No public floats available
   Temporary anchorage near any of the beaches, depending on the wind; overnight anchorage in a small cove behind Chads Island,[1] though ferry wash makes this spot uncomfortable; or in the bay by the Tortoise Islets,[2] except during a southerly wind

Facilities On Portland Island, none
   At Tsehum Harbour about 3 miles southwest of Portland Island, complete marina services
   At Fulford Harbour, Saltspring Island,[4] fuel and water at the public wharf near the ferry landing; phone and toilets, groceries and post office and cafe nearby

Caution Approach Portland Island paying attention to your chart: the surrounding waters hold many shoals and reefs. Remember to take the currents into account.

Access By boat only to Portland Island
   Launching ramps at many sites along the Saanich Peninsula, within a 5-mile range of Portland Island

The shoreline looped and indented, a series of bays, each one quite different. A sandy beach in the next bay east of the Chads Island anchorage, and another facing Brackman Island[3] to the south. A gravel and smoothly worn rock beach by the southern anchorage.

Sheep and deer have worn trails all over the island, the sheep leaving tufts of wool along their favourite routes. They follow the cliffs; they wander through arbutus groves and over mossy rocks, ferns and wild mushrooms; they crisscross the island through surprisingly dense stands of evergreens and waist-high salal. The sheep are as shy as the deer, but are curious. Walk quietly to see them feeding in the open fields.

Portland Island was once owned by Major-General "One-Arm" Sutton, a colourful character who bought the island with his winnings from the Calcutta Derby Sweeps, and lived here in grand style with his race horses. Below the substantial barn he built near the southeast side of the island, an orchard of plum and pear trees, fuzzy with Old Man's Beard and other ghostly mosses. Along the grass slopes by the beach, the remains of a cabin site, and rotting boat timbers barely held together with large squared boat nails: perfect picnic sites under huge oak trees.

A field, sixty-five acres of cleared land, cuts a strip right across the island. Spend hours poking about in the ruins of the old settlements. A house which once must have been beautiful has been stripped and despoiled, and blackberry bushes grow through the window spaces. Around the house, rose bushes, crabapple trees, fences and gardens. And hidden in the grass near the collapsed sheds, a tiny tombstone states, simply, FLOSS.

Did you know: The British Columbia government gave the island to Princess Margaret during the 1958 centennial celebrations. She gave it back, and the provincial government designated the island a marine park.

Provincial Marine Parks in the Gulf Islands

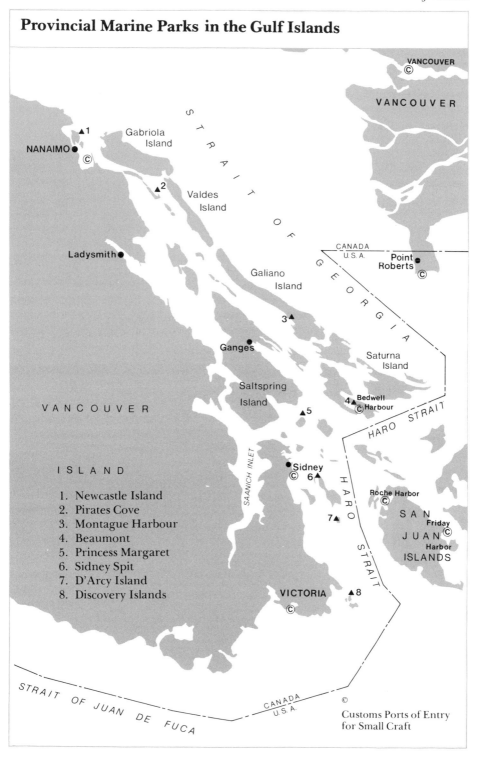

VANCOUVER Ⓒ

VANCOUVER

▲1 Gabriola
Island

NANAIMO● Ⓒ

▲2 Valdes
Island

STRAIT OF GEORGIA

Ladysmith●

CANADA
U.S.A.

Point
Roberts
Ⓒ

Galiano
Island

3▲

Ganges●

Saturna
Island

Saltspring
Island

4▲ Bedwell
Ⓒ Harbour

▲5

HARO STRAIT

VANCOUVER

SAANICH INLET

●Sidney
Ⓒ 6▲

HARO STRAIT

Roche Harbor
Ⓒ

ISLAND

SAN

7▲

JUAN

Friday
Ⓒ

1. Newcastle Island
2. Pirates Cove
3. Montague Harbour
4. Beaumont
5. Princess Margaret
6. Sidney Spit
7. D'Arcy Island
8. Discovery Islands

Harbor
ISLANDS

VICTORIA●
Ⓒ

▲8

STRAIT OF JUAN DE FUCA

CANADA
U.S.A.

Ⓒ Customs Ports of Entry
for Small Craft

95

Up-ended rock at Bedwell Harbour

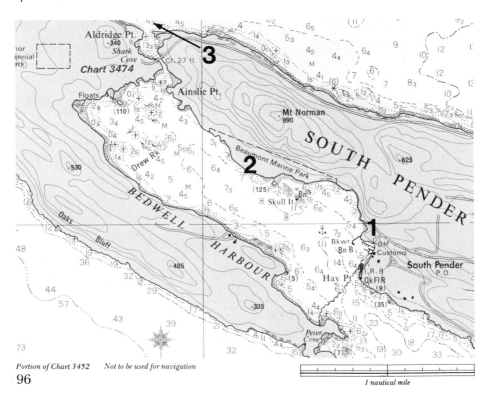

21

Bedwell Harbour and Beaumont Marine Park

What's There convenient Port of Entry when coming from the San Juan Islands....fishing....small-boat camping....swimming pool....waterfront lounge....mink, otter, seals....

Charts

3474 Bedwell Harbour and Port Browning	1:12,000
3310 small craft charts of Gulf Islands	1:40,000
3452 Haro Strait to Stuart Channel	1:40,000

Moorage Marine and public floats at South Pender[1]

At Beaumont Marine Park,[2] good anchorage in the bay behind Skull Islet; mooring buoys

Facilities At South Pender, Canada Customs, marina and resort facilities including general store, laundry and showers, restaurant, accommodation, heated swimming pool, charts

Caution The pass between North and South Pender Islands is navigable to many boats, with care. Tidal currents up to 4 knots flood northward to Port Browning. Watch for the fixed highway bridge with clearance of 8.2 metres (27 feet) with bridge supports in the middle of the stream. And watch for kelp beds and drying rocks.

The pass has a least depth of 2.1 metres (7 feet), and the navigable channel is marked with spar buoys.

Access Car access to South Pender via car ferry from Swartz Bay or from Tsawwassen, to Otter Bay on North Pender

Launching ramp: Port Browning

Bedwell Harbour for roughing it. Or for cruising in style. Either way, the choices are intriguing. Swim from a beach, or in a heated pool. Cook at a campground fire pit, or dress yourself up and dine out. Sit under a magnificent Garry oak on the promontory of the park to watch a sunset. Or watch from a window seat of the waterfront lounge.

Convenient: through customs at South Pender, pick up supplies, and then a moment later moored at the marine park. All in one protected bay. Or through the canal to another bay!

Beaumont Marine Park is perfect for small-boat camping: beach a boat easily on the sand and gravel shore, and campsites are only a few steps away. Gather clams and crabs within the harbour, and fish for salmon at the harbour mouth. Having no luck with salmon, try cooking the dog fish that you're sure to catch. Failing even that, there's the marina store with a varied stock: everything you need to stay a weekend, or a week.

Some strange rock formations in the park. Conglomerate boulders stand like free-form sculpture, or like stubby totem poles. Gravel gives way to up-ended layers of rock that have worn smooth in rows and ridges, like monster backbones draped across the shore.

A trail in the park is a forest tour. Stands of pine smell of hot dry days. An alder grove full of birds' nests. Alligatored bark of Garry oak in side-by-side contrast with the soap-smooth skin of arbutus. Behind the campsites, a damp gully filled with cedar shade and cedar fragrance.

Did you know: North Pender and South Pender were once one island: the channel between them was man-made in 1903.

About Dogfish

Dogfish are a curious species of fish: no bones, no ribs; a skeleton of cartilage and a skin like rubberized sandpaper. Rows of frightfully sharp teeth. An identifying spike along each dorsal fin. All together, a prickly customer, and by the way it takes bait, a personality to match.

Dogfish are usually caught by default, like summer colds; and like colds, they are more a nuisance than a danger. The little sharks are harder to avoid than they are to catch. They range from California to Alaska, sometimes travelling in packs of thousands. The young are born alive after a gestation period of almost two years. They grow slowly and live a long time, sometimes thirty years. The females can weigh nine kilograms (twenty pounds) but the males are generally smaller.

Indians used dogfish oil both as food and for lamps, loggers used the oil to grease their skids, and in the 1940s dogfish formed the basis of a multi-million dollar industry, the livers being the main source of Vitamin A. After the war the vitamin was synthesized and dogfish, once hunted to scarcity, again multiplied to nuisance proportions. Now the dogfish is slowly gaining acceptance as a food fish. One small "catch" to this catch: the flesh contains small amounts of urea which causes an unpleasant smell during storage or cooking. Marinating solves this problem. The British have been dealing with dogfish for years: they call it "flake" and serve it in their fish and chips.

Try dogfish:
>Dress down the fish as soon as it is caught.
>Peel the skin off the meat.
>Cut the meat into fillets or steaks.
>Cover the pieces with a marinade of water and lemon juice or vinegar: about one cup of water and one tablespoon of lemon juice or vinegar for each pound of fish.
>Let soak overnight.
>Then use the fish, white and firm and tasty, as any other. Why not Shark Steaks?

Rounding Nose Point out of Long Harbour

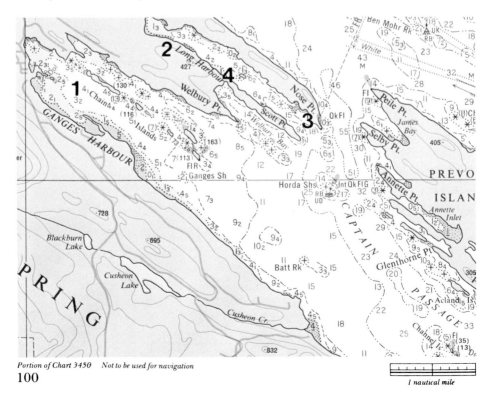

1 nautical mile

22

Captain Passage

What's There a comprehensive island community....resorts and marinas....undeveloped shorelines....great choice of great anchorages....good seafood foraging....pink rhodonite....

Charts

3470 Ganges Harbour and Long Harbour	1:18,000
3310 small craft charts of Gulf Islands	1:40,000
3452 Haro Strait to Stuart Channel	1:40,000

Moorage In Ganges Harbour,[1] public floats protected by a breakwater, guest moorage at marinas

Good anchorage in various nooks and hideaways in Ganges Harbour, in Long Harbour,[2] and in the inlets of Prevost Island

Facilities None on the Prevost Island side of the channel

At Ganges, most marina and repair facilities; medical services and the only hospital on the islands; various retail outlets, including pharmacy, liquor store, grocery stores and a hardware store, charts

Caution The tidal currents in Captain Passage flood north at rates up to 3-4 knots, and may cause tide rips near Nose Point.[3]

Watch for seaplanes landing in Ganges Harbour.

Access By boat only to Prevost Island; car access to Saltspring Island via car ferry service from Crofton to Vesuvius Bay, from Swartz Bay to Fulford Harbour, and from Tsawwassen, on the mainland, to Long Harbour

Launching ramp: Ganges Harbour; a carry path[4] to portage small boats between Welbury Bay and Long Harbour

The Saltspring Island side of Captain Passage is settled and civilized, the Prevost Island side mostly natural, and both sides indented with a surprising number of shoreline miles to explore. Pretty shores and protected waters, with all the facilities of Ganges as a bonus.

The Ganges wharf is a busy parking lot of boats in summer. It's fun just to wander through the town, for many of the buildings are old and interesting. Browse the specialty shops for antiques, for cottage crafts and books. Stop a while at the really pleasant community park by the wharf and look through pamphlets obtained from the tourist bureau just a step from where you sit.

At Long Harbour, some of the calmest anchorages in the area. Waterfront homes, a luxurious yacht club outstation, a ferry landing, and the green grounds of a resort. But also miles of terraced bluffs and little pocket beaches.

For more seclusion, go to the Prevost Island side of the passage, to James Bay, Selby Cove, Annette Inlet, or Glenthorn Passage. Much of the shore is "No Trespassing", but catch glimpses of orchards and gardens and cattle, and even more of evergreens, arbutus, and wildlife. Seals sunning on the rocks. A large blue heron, feathers like a patriarch's beard, roosting above a tidepool.

At low tide dig for seaworms as large as snakes to use as bait for bottom fish you didn't know existed. The crabbing here is excellent. Clams, too, and even oysters.

A garden of seaside vegetables grows on the intertidal shore. With the help of a field guide to edible plants, gather dusty-looking orach, so fresh and salty tasting. Seaside plantain grows in clumps of fleshy long blades: its common name is goose-tongue. And glasswort, commonly called "chicken-claws", is unmistakable. Just pick the topmost tender parts of this plant; the rest is stringy. Gather up a salad of wild greens!

Did you know: Some of the first settlers on Saltspring Island were Negroes from California, who bought their freedom and came north to start a new life.

A Salad of Seaside Edibles

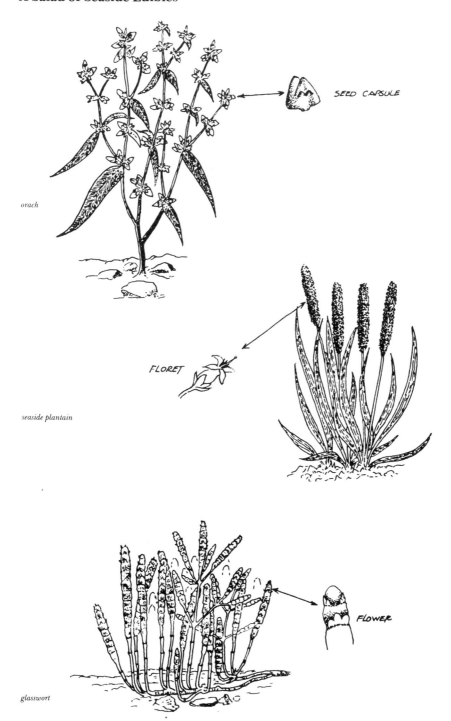

orach

SEED CAPSULE

FLORET

seaside plantain

glasswort

FLOWER

Dogwood, tugs, and pleasure boats at Maple Bay

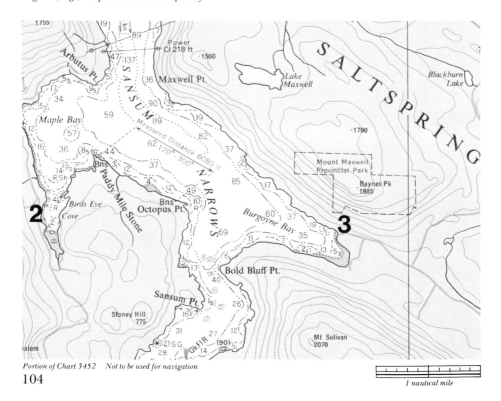

Portion of Chart 3452   Not to be used for navigation

1 nautical mile

23

Sansum Narrows

What's There country walks....swimming....good crabbing....year-round salmon fishing....Cowichan Indian knitwear....

Charts
3310 small craft charts of Gulf Islands   1:40,000
3452 Haro Strait to Stuart Channel   1:40,000

Moorage At Maple Bay,[1] a public wharf
At Birds Eye Cove,[2] marina floats and anchorage
Landing float and anchorage on mud bottom in Burgoyne Bay[3] on Saltspring Island

Facilities None in Burgoyne Bay
At Birds Eye Cove, extensive marina facilities and cruising supplies; showers and laundry, restaurant, post office, groceries, charts
At Maple Bay, a general store by the wharf

Caution Whirlpools and tide rips may occur in Sansum Narrows, but generally the current does not exceed 3 knots.

Access Road access to Maple Bay and to Birds Eye Cove; to Burgoyne Bay via car ferry from Crofton to Vesuvius Bay, from Swartz Bay to Fulford Harbour, or from Tsawwassen to Long Harbour
Launching ramps: Maple Bay[1] and at Maple Bay Marina[2]

Some people like to fish in Sansum Narrows. Some like to anchor quietly in Burgoyne Bay. Others like the extensive marina facilities at Birds Eye Cove. This area has something for everyone, at any time of year.

In Burgoyne Bay expect Dungeness crab of legal size in an overnight net. Crab we count on. But ling cod? In a crab net? One setting yielded three small rock fish and several crabs. We left them in the net and lowered it again. When next we hauled up the crab net, one small rock fish had escaped, but in its place was a five-pound ling cod. Incredible fishing in Burgoyne Bay!

Children like the little rock beach near the public wharf because of the weird and wonderful things to find at low tide. The anchorage in front of the beach is surprisingly deep: a hole, in fact. And a cod hole at that. Drop a line over to catch supper while watching your children on the beach. Good swimming at the head of the bay when the long expanse of sand warms the incoming tide.

The view of Mount Maxwell from the bay is splendid: the view from the top of Mount Maxwell is spectacular. Watch for hang gliders jumping from the peak and drifting down to the fields.

Saltspring Island's Burgoyne Valley is one of those very walkable areas with roads pleasantly rural and the traffic usually light. The road follows the valley with no real uphills and downhills, but just three miles of fields and farms. Sheep follow you along the fences, and wild rabbits dash from roadside bushes.

During summer weekends, navigation through Sansum Narrows can be a challenge. Dozens of trollers fishing their individual circuits or just drifting easily on the current. Tugs pulling barges and booms, short-hauled, through the channel. Other boats just passing through on their way to somewhere else. And sailboats can usually count on wind for a spinnaker run.

In Maple Bay, a change of pace. Buy or sell a boat at the marina. Buy anything from beans to bottom paint or — a good purchase for wintertime sailors — a warm wool toque knitted by the local Cowichan Indians. Do laundry. Or dine in Polynesian splendour at the restaurant near the marina. Stop during a winter cruise for a hot shower in a freezing-cold outside cubicle: an exhilarating experience.

Did you know: Like many small islands near old village sites, Burial Islet used to be an Indian graveyard.

Hot Crab in a Pinch

Freshly caught and freshly cooked crab picked right from the shell and eaten with chunks of crusty bread and a cool white wine needs nothing more said about it. But if your catch was so small that you must stretch a bit of crab meat a long way to make a meal, or if your catch was so large that you have a little crab meat left over for lunch next day, try it done this simple way:

> Crab meat from 1 large Dungeness crab or from two rock crabs: about a cupful
> 1 10-ounce can of cream of mushroom or cream of celery soup
> 2 tablespoons mayonnaise
> 1 teaspoon curry powder
> Garnish: parsley or a sprinkling of paprika
> Toast, or toasted muffins, or thin pancakes

Heat together the soup, mayonnaise and curry in the top of a double boiler, or in any pot set within a larger pot of boiling water. Stir until sauce is smooth and hot. Add crab, and heat for a few minutes longer. Serve over hot toast, muffins, or pancakes.

Serves 2 hungry people. Or more.

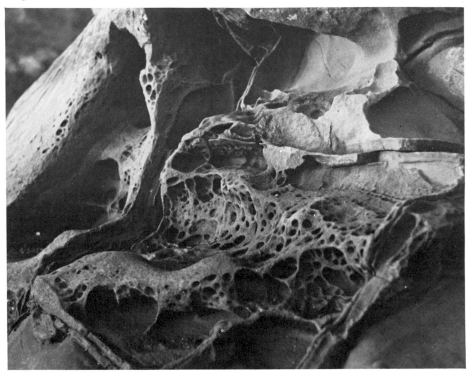

Sandstone lace at Pirates Cove

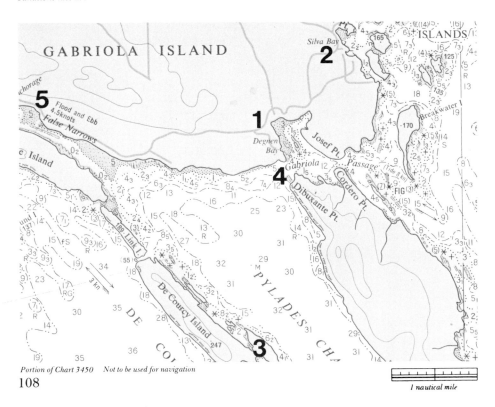

1 nautical mile

24

Silva Bay to Pirates Cove Marine Park

What's There resort and marine park....exciting current passages....waterfront neighbourhood pub....island walks....small-boat camping....fishing....carved sandstone formations....Indian petroglyph....wreck of the *Thrasher* at Thrasher Rock....

Charts

3310 small craft charts of Gulf Islands	1:40,000
3453 Trincomali and Stuart Channels	1:40,000

Moorage In Degnen Bay,[1] a public wharf and anchorage
    At Silva Bay,[2] marina floats and anchorage
    At Pirates Cove,[3] anchorage only, with landing floats for dinghies

Facilities In Degnen Bay, no facilities
    At Silva Bay, complete cruising and resort services: shipyard, boat and bicycle rentals, laundry, showers, groceries
    Pirates Cove Marine Park: picnic sites and walk-in campsites, pit toilets, trails, drinking water from a hand pump

Caution Tidal currents in Gabriola Passage[4] may reach 8 knots: best to go through at slack water. Watch for tugboats with tows coming through the narrow channel.

Access By boat only to Pirates Cove Marine Park; car access to Degnen Bay and to Silva Bay via car ferry from Nanaimo to Descanso Bay on northern Gabriola Island
    Launching ramp: Silva Bay

A bit of everything for any kind of boating. Pirates Cove for anchorage at a marine park and for small-boat camping. Degnen Bay for landing at a public wharf where the locals keep their boats. And Silva Bay for a touch of luxury.

Pirates Cove Marine Park is sometimes so crowded on a summer weekend that the boats must raft together at anchor, but in winter see the park in a different light entirely. Where summer children played on the pebble beach outside the cove, a winter seal made eyes at us. Arbutus trees bright with winter berries and loud with feeding crows. A picnic in Gulf Island winter sunshine and a walk along silent trails. On the south side of the park, a deer grazing near the long-handled water pump. It's a lovely park in any season.

The shores of Pylades Channel display their sandstone shapes. Burst bubbles improbably lacy. Great weathered knobs and convoluted scoops. Shadowy hollows large enough to lie in.

As the back door between Nanaimo and Pylades Channel, False Narrows[5] is a salt-water creek, slow and shallow. But Gabriola Passage, though actually easy and a short spurt through at slack water, can be an excitement of overfalls, upwells and backwashes. A boat seems to slide to shore, the water in the middle of the passage seems to heap up higher and higher. Follow the eddies to feel the current grip and lose its hold.

In Degnen Bay, look for a petroglyph, for an Indian rock carving, on a sandstone outcropping at the high tide mark. Walk to Silva Bay for an evening at the neighbourhood pub. Come back in the dark, to discover that a sky full of stars does nothing to lighten a country road. But a lovely place to be lost, with sheep bleating softly in the fields, and the scent of garden flowers heavy in the night.

Ply the passage from Degnen Bay to Silva Bay through the rock pile of reefs, the floats of kelp beds, and the split of narrow channels. If cold and drenched on rainy days and rough crossings, glory in the swirl pool and sauna at the Silva Bay Resort while drying your gear at the laundromat. On a warm and sunny day rent bicycles at the resort and tour the easy-wheeling roads of Gabriola Island.

Silva Bay is almost geographically perfect for boaters. A calm and sheltered refuge where you want it most. A perfect landfall and a perfect place to sit and wait for the right conditions before crossing the Strait of Georgia. Then, passing Thrasher Rock Light on Gabriola Reefs, head out toward the Fraser, to Vancouver, or to Howe Sound.

Did you know: De Courcy Island used to be the site of Brother Twelve's colony, a strange sect which in the 1930s built a farm complete with gun emplacements to discourage visitors.

Names that Rubbed Off

The names of some of the rocks and reefs and points in the Gulf Islands commemorate some of the ships that struck them. Some ships found uncharted rocks. Some were sailing ships heavily laden with coal out of Comox, Ladysmith and Nanaimo, and wrecked on the site. And some ships struck but escaped, leaving only a name at the site.

Two at least left names on places which had never been named before. A small but shallow patch in the middle of Captain Passage was unknown until 1901 when hit by a Norwegian steamer, but known thenceforth as Horda Shoals. And in Trincomali Channel, Ben Mohr Rock was "discovered" by a British vessel which grated over it.

Coal-filled sailing ships were at the mercy of the tugs that towed them through the narrow Gulf Island channels. On a summer evening in 1880, the *Thrasher*, off Gabriola Reefs and carrying 2600 tons of coal, struck an outlying rock which the light-draft towing boats had easily cleared: the hulk and her cargo of coal can still be seen by divers. During a vicious gale in 1874 the *Panther*'s tug, fighting for life in the storm, was forced to cut free, and the 194-foot *Panther* broke up on the southern point of Wallace Island. The bark *John Rosenfeld* was deep and heavy with a record load when towed onto a rock in Tumbo Reef in 1886, and grounded so securely that the tug could not free her.

Not every ship left its bones where it left its name. The *Rosedale*, holed near Race Rocks on her approach to Victoria in 1862, was beached in Ross Bay. And a few months later the *Alpha*, driven onto an islet near Discovery Island during a snowstorm, discharged her cargo and floated off again.

Sea Bird Point, Discovery Island, surprisingly owes its name not to the birds that guard it, but to an American paddle steamer run aground here in 1858. More obvious link between rock and wreck: Miami Islet, named for the steel steamship which in 1900 struck bottom halfway between Thetis Island and Danger Reefs, and still shows at tides below 3.4 metres (11 feet): a graphic warning to all boaters.

Chapter Four
Vancouver Area

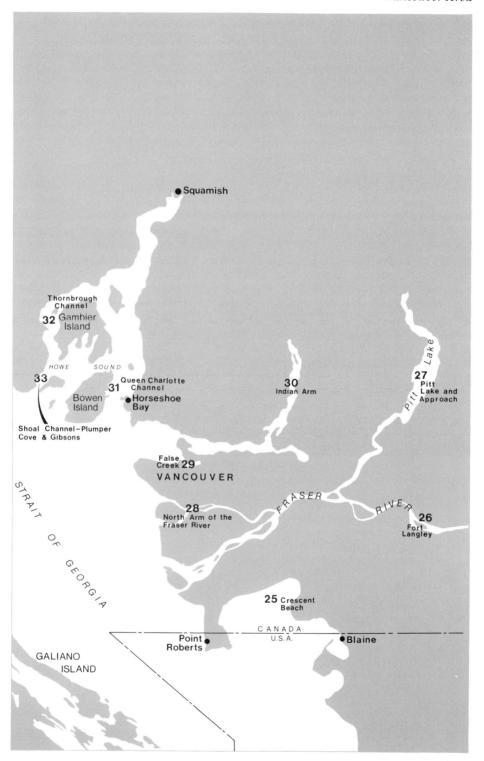

● Squamish

Thornbrough Channel

32 Gambier Island

HOWE   SOUND

33

Queen Charlotte Channel

31

Bowen Island

● Horseshoe Bay

Shoal Channel – Plumper Cove & Gibsons

30 Indian Arm

Pitt Lake

27 Pitt Lake and Approach

False Creek 29

VANCOUVER

FRASER

RIVER

28

North Arm of the Fraser River

26 Fort Langley

STRAIT   OF   GEORGIA

25 Crescent Beach

CANADA
U.S.A.

● Point Roberts

● Blaine

GALIANO ISLAND

Grass, sand, and shade at Crescent Beach

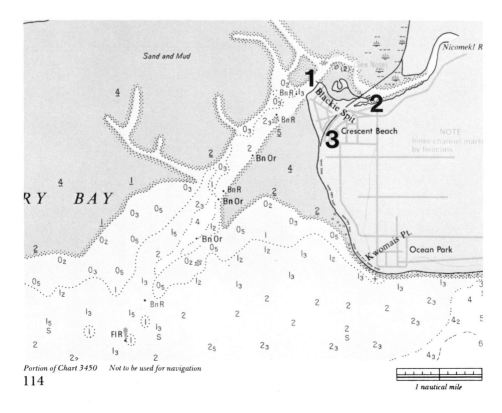

Portion of Chart 3450   Not to be used for navigation

1 nautical mile

25

Crescent Beach

What's There sandy beaches and sand dunes....loop walk....concession stands....crabbing....salmon fishing off Point Roberts....International Boundary....blue herons....good place to careen a sailboat....

Charts

3450 East Point to Sand Heads   1:80,000

Moorage At Blackie Spit,[1] a public wharf with a small float

At the mouth of the Nikomekl River, visitors' moorage at a marina[2]

Facilities Complete marina facilities

At Crescent Beach village,[3] groceries, cafes, bakery with tea room, and various specialty shops

Caution Follow the piling markers closely to stay within the dredged channel and proceed slowly. Advisable, if in a keel boat, to negotiate the shallow channels only during a rising tide.

Bridges The Burlington Northern railway bridge has a minimum clearance of about 3 metres (10 feet) under its closed swing span. A bridge keeper is generally on duty from 0800 to 2100 during the cruise season. For off-season and for extra-early openings, check with the Crescent Beach Marina (604-531-7551) the day before to make arrangements.

Access By boat or car

Launching ramp: Crescent Beach Marina[2]

Four miles from shore the markers start, picking out a channel through mudbanks and sandbars. This shallow-water cruise has attractions of its own. Shallow water means warm water for swimming, and the beaches here are popular in summer. Sand, lifeguards, concession stands: Crescent Beach is a proper beachside blend of businesses and parks, of lawns and driftwood logs, of salt air and french fries.

Low tides bare the bars for miles and, even though Boundary Bay is a shellfish restricted area, the uncovered ground is fascinating to explore. A warning: returning tides come in quickly and with force. Don't let yourself be stranded.

Try a pleasant hour's walking tour of Crescent Beach. From the marina, a shady trail dips under the railway trestle and leads, single file, around the sloughs. Walk quietly. Watch the great blue herons hunting, and the wild ducks feeding among the reeds. The trail rounds an open sandy point; soft sand, to walk barefoot. Here, a sailboat careened and freshly bottom painted. A wild rabbit scuttling into cover. A rider putting her horse through its paces along the shore. Beyond this point the trail becomes a road: past the public wharf, past the beach area and to the village park with its petroglyph, that granite boulder pecked out with face-shapes by some ancient tribe.

Beyond the marina the Nikomekl River is a small and quiet stream, still navigable for many boats. The river winds between fields and dykes to fishermen's mooring floats about half a mile upstream. Explore the stream at sunset, at a quiet hour. A canoe comes up from behind. A man walks his dog along the dyke. A flock of blue herons fly to their night-time roosts. A very peaceful place.

Did you know: In 1792 Dionisio Alcala Galiano named Boundary Bay Ensanada del Engano: the Creek of Deception.

Recipes with a Grain of Salt

The best galley recipes are those that can be adapted, adjusted, and generally fooled about with. Rarely on a boat do you have all the ingredients called for: you must use stand-ins for some ingredients and leave others out altogether: you end with a dish that might as well have been invented on the spot. The fun of cooking.

For instance, start with the idea of spaghetti and meat balls and let chunks of freshly caught rock cod stand proxy for meat. For tomato sauce, fry a sliced onion until it's transparent, add a can of stewed tomatoes, and spice to taste with whatever comes to hand: salt, pepper, chile pepper flakes, barbecue sauce, parsley flakes, or a generous dollop of ketchup which also thickens the sauce. Add the cod, and let simmer until the fish is cooked, about 10 or 15 minutes. Serve the whole business over spaghetti. Or why not over cooked rice?

Also a wonderfully adaptable recipe:

Poisson en Papillote

Seafood fillets of cod, or sole, or salmon; or crab meat or deveined shrimp or a combination

Vegetables one or several of sliced tomatoes, green beans, sliced carrots, onions, mushrooms, zucchini....whatever's available

Liquid white wine, or beer, or soya sauce, or oil and vinegar salad dressing, or....

Optional a slice of cheese for each serving

Having chosen your ingredients, make a foil packet for each person. Keep the shiny side of the foil inward and use two layers if not using heavy duty foil. In each packet arrange a serving of seafood, a layer of vegetables, and about two tablespoons of liquid. Top with a slice of cheese, if you wish. Seal the packets carefully. Place over heat — on a barbecue or hibachi, among the hot coals of a campfire, or in an oven — until the vegetables are done and the fish will flake easily, about 20 minutes.

Serve right in the foil packets. No plates to wash!

Fort Langley National Historic Park on the Fraser River

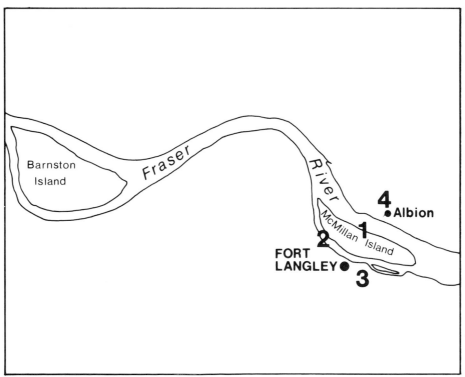

Not to be used for navigation

1 nautical mile

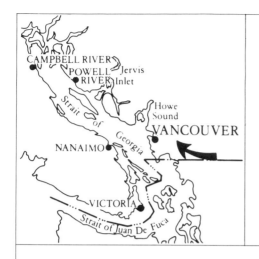

26

Fort Langley

What's There a trip up-river in the wake of the fur traders....Fort Langley National Historical Park....museums....riverside dining....sturgeon fishing....farms and fishboats....

Charts
3488 Fraser River, Sand Heads to Douglas Island 1:25,000
No soundings charted past Douglas Island

Moorage Near the ferry landing,[1] a public wharf with floats
Anchorage in Bedford Channel[2] when the water level is high enough
The passage behind the east end of McMillan Island has been dredged to accommodate tugs, but the water shoals rapidly on the island side of the channel and toward the bridge

Facilities At Fort Langley,[3] groceries and general supplies, waterfront restaurant
At Albion,[4] fuel, water and groceries; shipyards
Boat-supply businesses along the Fraser River above New Westminster are geared toward serving commercial boats: this is more a work area than a tourist area.

Caution Extra care needed for river navigation: floating debris is difficult to see in the murky water, sand bars shift from year to year, and during summer freshets the current may exceed 7 knots. The worst of the flood force is usually over by August. Check: does your boat insurance cover navigation past the chart soundings on the Fraser River?

Note: Tidal water fishing regulations are in effect to the Canadian Pacific railway bridge at Mission.

Access By boat or car; free car ferry service between Albion and McMillan Island
Launching ramps: Bedford Channel; Albion

The Fraser was a river of riches, a royal road for traders of fur and gold and salmon. Trading and defence were the reasons for the Hudson's Bay Company's building Fort Langley, and the Fort is now an historical park. Going there by boat brings history to life. As the traders did, you work the long up-current miles, and you anchor, as they also did, in the shadows of the palisades.

The fort is fascinating — in one building a carpenter in pioneer costume, himself a part of the display, works with hand tools to re-build worn parts of other displays. Watch him fashion a wooden bucket, a wagon wheel, a work bench. Chips fly, and the scent of shavings is very sharp. In fact, scent plays a part in all the exhibits. In the store house, close your eyes and breathe deeply. A marvellous mixture of smells here: plug tobacco, castile soap, dried fish and candle wax.

Run your fingers through the furs stacked on the counter. Notice the fur press that can make bales of furs weighing over a hundred pounds. And notice the sundial that kept men on company time: twelve hours a day.

From the bastion look at the river. In the 1800s ocean-going ships swung at anchor here to take on cargoes of cranberries for San Francisco, furs for England, and salted salmon for Hawaii and Australia.

Many of the place names in the area are related to the history of Fort Langley. The fort cooperage made the barrels in which the salt fish was packed, and wood for the barrel staves came, naturally, from the shoreline of Stave Lake. And Kanaka Creek was named for the Hawaiian Islanders, the Kanakas, working for the Hudson's Bay Company and settling in the area. And McMillan Island, named after James McMillan, a Chief Factor of the company.

Across the street from the Fort, the Langley Museum and the Farm Museum. Three museums in one small town: a cruise not so much to a place as to another time!

Did you know: When the water level was high enough, and the current not too strong, boats navigated as far as Yale, more than a hundred miles from the river mouth.

Samson V

Snag-puller. River roustabout. Surprising sight among sleek ocean freighters and modern river tugs. The steam-puffing stern-wheeler *Samson V* threads history as she threads the Fraser River channels. Built in 1937, the vessel is the fifth of a series of sturdy little workers that since 1883 have helped to keep the Fraser safe for boats: surveying the ever-changing channels; servicing the channel markers; and, with the hoist poised over the bows, pulling obstructions from the navigation routes.

Samson V is maneuverable enough to turn in her own length. At 1.37 metres (4½ feet), a shallow enough draft to clear sandbarred shallows. With 200 horsepower, powerful enough to fight the muddy summer freshet. She ranges the Fraser from Sand Heads to the reaches of the river above Mission, and along the North Arm and the length of the Pitt River. A joy to watch.

121

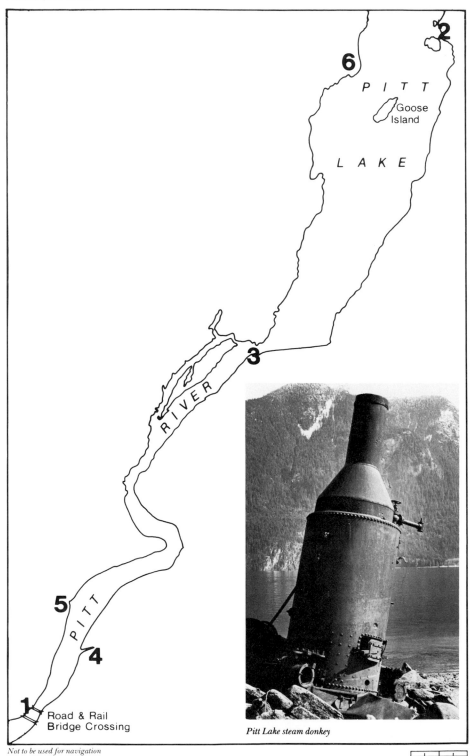

6

P I T T

Goose
Island

L A K E

2

3

R I V E R

5

P I T T

4

1
Road & Rail
Bridge Crossing

Pitt Lake steam donkey

1 nautical mile

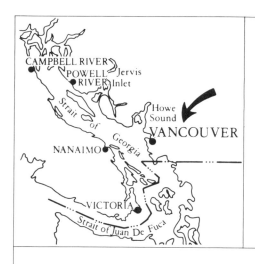

27

Pitt Lake and Approach

What's There fresh-water cruising accessible from salt water....pictographs....sandy beaches....spectacular waterfalls....undeveloped shorelines....birdwatching....a legend of lost gold....

Charts
3060 Pitt River   1:25,000
No soundings charted past the entrance to Pitt Lake

Moorage Public wharf,[1] old and run-down, near the railway bridge
Anchorage only, on Pitt Lake
Find the best protection from winds between Little Goose Island and the smaller island;[2] the latter is joined to the mainland by a rock bar

Facilities None, on Pitt Lake
Some marina services along Pitt River; canoe rentals near the Lougheed Highway bridge
Stock up on groceries and other necessities before coming to cruise here

Caution Winds rise quickly and can funnel down the lake with considerable force. Do not leave your boat unattended for long in an exposed anchorage.

Note: Non-tidal sport-fishing regulations are in effect upstream of the Canadian Pacific railway bridge on Pitt River.

Bridges Railway bridge clearance is 2.1 metre (7 feet) above Higher High Water (not valid during freshet); signal to open: 3 long blasts
Pitt River Highway Bridge, 3.6 metres (12 feet); 2 short and 2 long

Access Car access to Pitt Lake only as far as Grant Narrows[3]
Launching ramps: Alouette Marina;[4] Pitt River Boat Club;[5] Grant Narrows

Pitt Lake is wilderness water in a wilderness setting: a fresh-water fiord. Wonderful that such a place can be so easily reached by cruising boats.

This cruise really begins in the Pitt River which links the lake and the mighty Fraser River in thirteen easy-going miles. Near the bridges lies an ancient public wharf, and a block from that the Wild Duck Inn with pub and restaurant: a good place to gather local information, and local colour.

With its backwaters and long and winding tributaries, the Pitt River is popular with canoeists, but larger craft must follow the main channels. The shores are dyked, and the shallows marked by dolphins and log booms. Neat farms on both sides of the river — a little Holland. In fact, hundreds of acres of marshland came under production as part of the Netherlands Reclamation Project.

Farther north several low hills force the river into a wide sweep, and the water backs behind the dykes to form sloughs and marshes: a sanctuary where thousands of birds nest and feed. Widgeon, mallard, golden-eye. Snow geese, and the unmistakable Canada geese. Drift by, and listen.

Near the lake, the last traces of tidal influence peter out. The wind tastes less of sea and more of snow fields. Buoys mark the channel through the silted lower end of the lake, but beyond that the chart gives no more soundings. You are in uncharted waters, but navigation is no problem: the lake is so deep and so crystal clear that shallows, where they do occur, can be seen easily.

A study in contrasts. Stark cliffs start three thousand feet overhead and drop down so straight that you can bring your boat alongside rock without touching bottom. Liquid lines of water-carved rock. Waterfalls, white and spectacular. The turquoise green of glacial streams. Lumber camps old and new, and a few dozen summer cabins. Indian rock paintings[6] along the western shore, and a steam donkey, a real museum piece.

Sand is the real surprise in a lake that seems so utterly rocky. But sand there is, and lots of it: sand where streams empty; sand bottom almost anywhere you anchor; and sandy beaches, mile after mile.

Try gold panning in the gravel bars of the upper Pitt River: somewhere up there, the story goes, is a lost gold mine. The legend of Slumach's gold makes good lazy day reading while drifting on the lake.

Did you know: In 1906 convicts on Goose Island quarried rock to supply building stones for the B.C. Penitentiary at New Westminster and locally the island is called Pen Island.

Something to Try: Gold Panning

Glorious, glittering gold: the lure of it, the fun and the dreaming of it. A cruising placer miner needs just a few simple tools, many of them already on the boat. A gold pan is a small investment and available in many coastal hardware stores. A "clam gun" does service as a miner's shovel. A bailing bucket for carrying black sand back to the boat for further cleaning. Tweezers from the medical kit. And a pill jar in which to store the "colours".

Any number of streams emptying to the sea may bear gold. Not in nuggets, perhaps, but in specks and flakes, and they are still gold. Even many beaches bear gold, though wave action grinds the metal flour-fine — past easy recovery. Try those streams swift enough to carry gold down from secret sources. Gold is heavy, a fact that works in favour of miners. It settles out readily. Pan gravel that collects against large rocks, or against bedrock or hardpan: pan gravel bars inside the bend of a stream, or along the highwater levels; look for specks of gold in moss and in clumps of roots along the flood level of the stream.

There is a knack to panning, to the swirling and dipping that separates gold from gravel. First, drop a shovelful of gravel into the pan. Immerse the pan in water, in a quiet pool where the current can't wash fine gold away. Work your hands through the gravel, picking out larger stones and breaking up clumps of clay. Now tilt the pan slightly away, and swirl the water in it around. Lighter rocks will climb to the sides. Let them go. Refill with water as necessary, and keep working out the unwanted rocks.

With the tweezers pick up the gold nuggets and the flecks of gold and drop them into a small jar of water. A clear jar that lets the glitter through. A very satisfying sight! So they say. You may never see a nugget, but the theoretical possibility is vastly entertaining.

No gold? Then use your new gold pan for cooking up a good mess of rice and seafood.

Pitt Lake pictographs

Racing canoe near Musqueam Reserve, North Arm

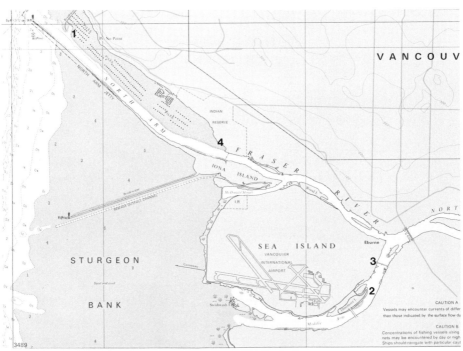

Portion of Chart 3480   Not to be used for navigation

1 nautical mile

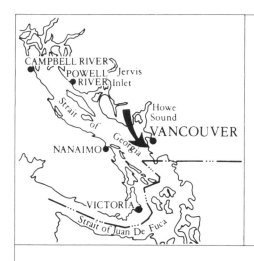

28

North Arm, Fraser River

What's There harbour seals....low-lying undeveloped delta island shores....Indian racing canoes....working tugboats, fishboats and boomboats....sawmills and sand dunes....elegant homes and golf courses....

Charts

3489 Fraser River, North Arm	1:18,000
3480 Active Pass to Burrard Inlet	1:50,000

Moorage Good anchorage in Fishermans Mooring Basin[1] at the outlet to North Arm

In the Middle Arm,[2] visitors' moorage at marinas and at the hotel

Facilities None, along the lower part of the Arm

In the Middle Arm, full marina services and a large hotel with waterfront restaurant

Caution A strong wind opposing the river current creates steep, rough seas near the shallow delta waters. In a small boat, head for shelter when the wind blows up. Watch for floating debris which is difficult to see in the murky water.

A warning about tying to log booms in Fishermans Mooring Basin: booms shift with the tides and can drag your boat into shallow waters, leaving it stranded at low tide. The basin shoals rapidly toward the pilings.

Note: The wash from your boat can be a hazard to men working on log booms in the narrow channel: please slow down.

Bridges Middle Arm Bridge[3] minimum clearance, about 7.5 metres (18 feet); signal to open: 4 long, 1 short. Bridge will not open during rush-hour traffic, 0700 to 0900, and 1600 to 1800.

Access By car to both shores of the North and Middle Arms

Launching ramps: Sea Island; Middle Arm

Though the North Arm of the Fraser River is the commercial route, this is a delightful channel to cruise. Drifting logs and the bad manners of those who make an unnecessarily big wash are really the only hazards to cruising: the rest is all pleasure.

Vancouver Harbour, and Wreck Beach with its nude sunbathers, are just around the corner. One minute you're cruising past city shores, then suddenly watching the city drop from sight, and right before you is the entrance to the North Arm.

A breakwater blocks out Fishermans Mooring Basin. The basin is a quiet spot to come for temporary shelter when you're fishing off Point Grey or Sturgeon Banks. Forty-knot winds can send spray surging over the breakwater rocks, but the basin is a calm place from which to watch for signs of better weather, and then, from which to make a dash out of the Arm.

Sightseeing, along the lower reaches of the channel: perhaps teams from the Musqueam Reserve[4] training in their remarkable racing canoes, horizontal forests of log booms, and golf course greens with borders of weeping willow. Behind those, glimpses of magnificent Marine Drive estates. On the opposite shore, long low sand dunes and wild flowers. And jets, soundless from here, floating down to the Vancouver International Airport on Sea Island.

Further up the channel the city reaches out with sawmills and factories and highway bridges high overhead. The Middle Arm offers marinas and the luxury of a large hotel with a waterfront restaurant. A nice choice, but why not picnic on delta sand dunes?

Did you know: By keeping Passage Island in range with Anvil Island you can safely clear the Fraser River delta shoals of Sturgeon Banks and Sand Heads: as noted by Captain George Vancouver in 1792.

About Sturgeon

A sturgeon isn't easily mistaken for anything else. Think of a fossil fish, a prehistoric leftover: armour-plated, snouty, and very very large. Add a sucker mouth; without teeth. Four whiskery feelers ahead of the mouth, and a scalloped ridge of spine.

Sturgeon are still taken from the Fraser River, but less commonly than in the past, and their average size is smaller. The fish are bottom scavengers often caught by accident on bottom-dragging lines. The bait to use is anything dead, and the deader the better. Eighty years ago a man caught an 1800-pound sturgeon at Mission and other people have caught fish weighing half a ton. Considering that sturgeon may live over fifty years, it isn't surprising that they grow so large. Fish less than three feet long must be thrown back.

Cleaning sturgeon is simple, with no scales to scrape. Just dress down the fish and consider its possibilities. The roe makes the very best caviar. The swim bladder was once used to make isinglass. But sturgeon flesh is lean and richly flavoured — a very desirable food, often featured in Chinese restaurants. Cut it into steaks about an inch thick. Trim off the skin. Boil it, broil it, bake it, or fry it, but especially grill it over the live coals of an hibachi. Sturgeon needs a longer cooking time than other fish, so watch that the outside doesn't dry before the inside is fully cooked. The flesh flakes easily when done. Serve with lemon butter.

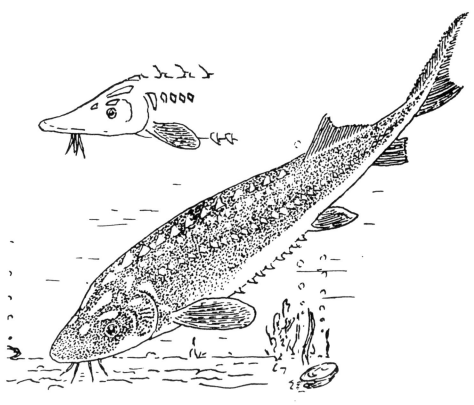

sturgeon

Moorage and city lights at False Creek

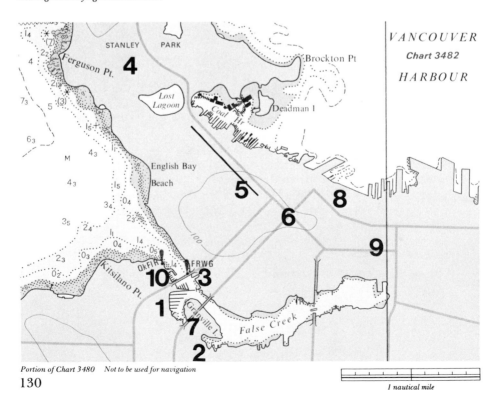

29

False Creek

What's There shoreside parks....Coast Guard Station....Vancouver city centre within walking distance....waterfront restaurants....Planetarium....Museum....Aquatic Centre....Maritime Museum....

Charts

3482 Vancouver Harbour, western portion	1:10,000
3481 Approaches to Vancouver Harbour	1:20,000

Moorage Temporary moorage at the civic marina,[1] the fishermen's floats or at marina floats

Limited anchorage in a small basin at the southeast end of Granville Island,[2] or near the end of False Creek out of the traffic channels

Do not anchor in the way of work boats

Facilities All marina supplies and facilities, and tourist services

At the Jib Set,[3] use of showers, laundry facilities, sauna and lounge included in price of overnight moorage; rentals and sailing lessons available

Caution Maximum speed in False Creek is 5 knots. Sails prohibited within the confines of the narrow channel.

Bridges Kitsilano railway bridge clearance, 4.6 metres (15 feet); signal to open: 3 long blasts. Manned 24 hours. The deepest channel is on the *west* side of the swing span; the east side is blocked by a drying sand bar.

Cambie Street bridge (Connaught Bridge), 12.8 metres (42 feet). Requires 4 hours notice to open: phone 327-8121.

Access Easy access by boat and by car

Launching ramp: near Vanier Park[10]

A cruise with a difference: to an inlet in the middle of a city, to a most convenient sort of street. Convenient, when you want a change of pace from roughing it, when you want to be near marina facilities for a re-fit or repairs, or when you simply want to be a boating tourist in a very beautiful city.

Stanley Park,[4] Robson Street,[5] Granville Mall[6] and Granville Island,[7] Gastown[8] and Chinatown[9] — all are within reasonable walking distance of False Creek moorage. And on rainy days without leaving the waterfront you can swim at the Aquatic Centre. At Vanier Park,[10] take in a show at the Planetarium, or spend an afternoon at the Maritime Museum where the *St. Roch,* first ship to complete the North West Passage both ways, is on display. Dine in splendour at a choice of waterside restaurants or anchor at the end of the inlet and scramble over to a "hamburger joint". A whiskery brown rat kept watch over our dinghy while we were ashore.

City rat or country rat? In False Creek, either. Within a hundred years the water has reflected virgin forest, sawmills, industry, and now, in a new phase of the cycle, parks and housing. Many changes since Captain G.H. Richards of the survey vessel *Plumper* explored the inlet in 1850, thinking it to be a creek mouth.

Yet for all the development, sea lions in the approach channel to False Creek; Canada geese along the bridge supports; and harbour seals surfacing silently among the hundreds of moored boats.

Did you know: The forty-seven-acre Granville Island, once little more than a sandbar, was built up from silt dredged from False Creek.

Provincial Marine Parks in the Vancouver Area

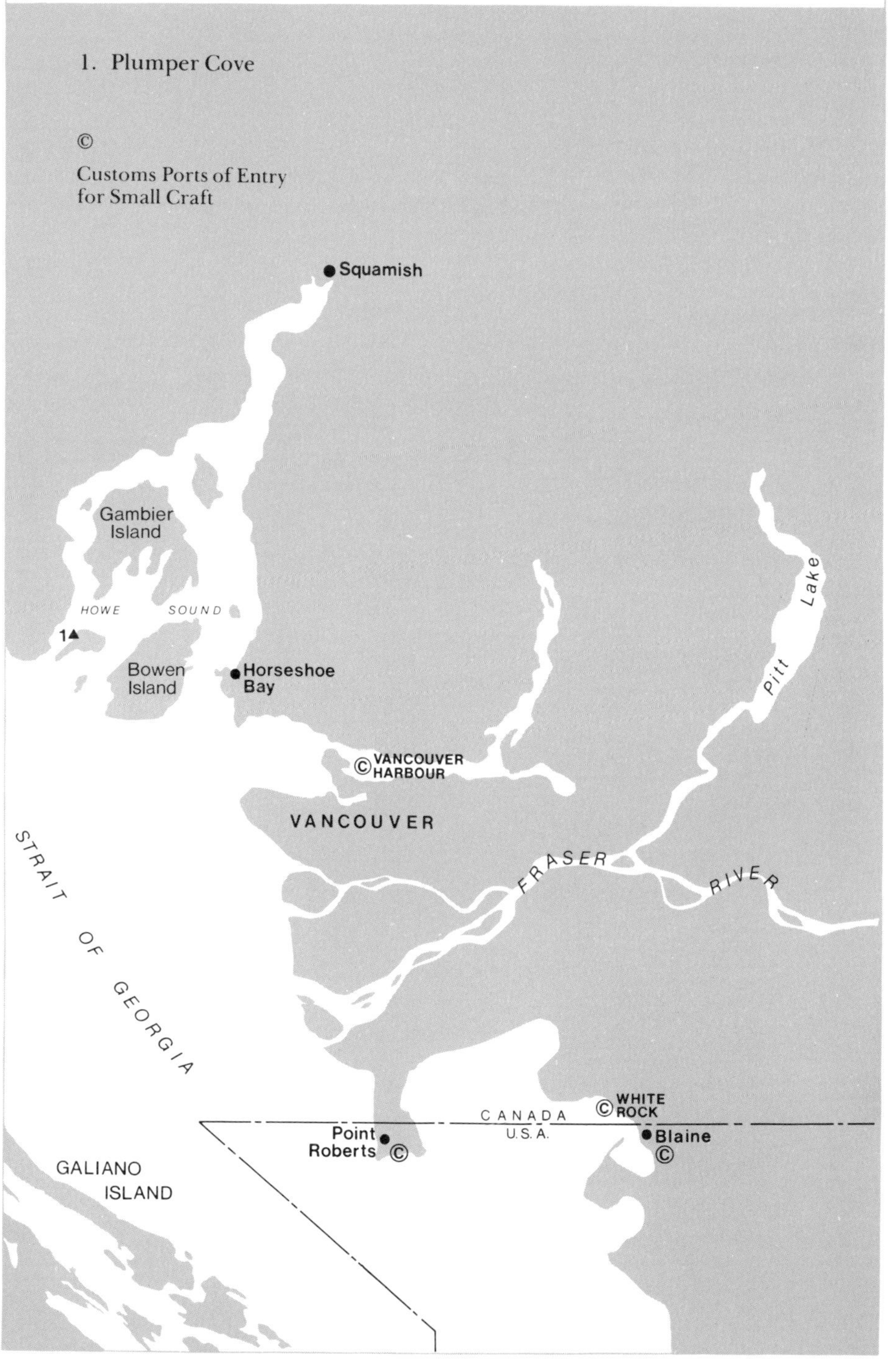

1. Plumper Cove

© Customs Ports of Entry for Small Craft

● Squamish

Gambier Island

HOWE   SOUND

1▲

Bowen Island

● Horseshoe Bay

© VANCOUVER HARBOUR

VANCOUVER

Pitt   Lake

FRASER   RIVER

STRAIT   OF   GEORGIA

GALIANO ISLAND

Point Roberts ©

CANADA
U.S.A.

© WHITE ROCK

● Blaine
©

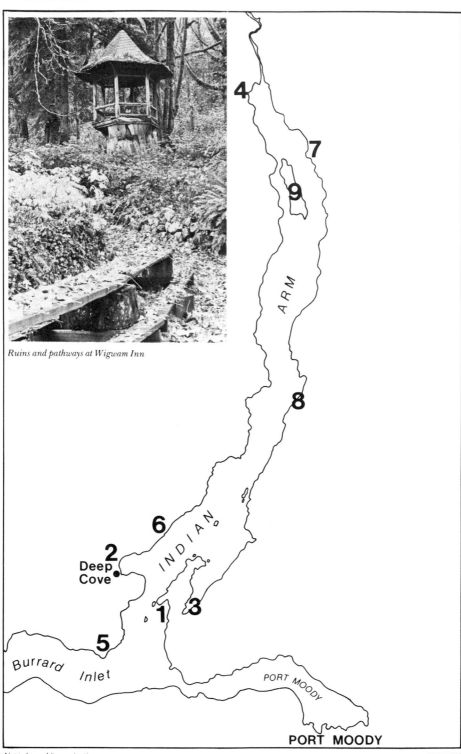

Ruins and pathways at Wigwam Inn

ARM

INDIAN

Deep Cove •

PORT MOODY

PORT MOODY

Burrard Inlet

1 nautical mile

30

Indian Arm

What's There wilderness shoreline of mountains and waterfalls....fishing....Dungeness crabs....wildlife....picnic sites....old logging claims and quarries....intriguing Wigwam Inn, a ruin being re-built....for scuba divers, a wreck in Bedwell Bay....

Charts

3435 Indian Arm   1:24,300

Moorage At Belcarra Park,[1] a public wharf and anchorage
At Deep Cove,[2] a public wharf, marina floats, and anchorage
Good anchorage in Bedwell Bay[3]
At Wigwam Inn,[4] $3 minimum to tie up; temporary anchorage nearby

Facilities General supplies and marina services at Deep Cove
Picnic sites at Cates Park,[5] Belcarra Park and at Wigwam Inn

Caution After heavy rains debris washes into the Arm from Indian River: watch for floating logs and deadheads hidden in the silty water. Choose anchorages with a thought to the strong and sudden winds that may blow down the inlet.

Access Car access to Bedwell Bay on one side, and to Woodlands[6] on the other side of Indian Arm; to Wigwam Inn by boat only
A Harbour Ferries cruise on Sundays and Wednesdays tours Indian Arm as far as Granite Falls,[7] with a 2-hour layover at Belcarra Park. Phone 687-9558
Launching ramps: Cates Park; Deep Cove Marina

A cruise here need not depend on weather. Indian Arm is undeniably beautiful in sunshine but even more spectacular in rain. Then Fairy Falls thunders over granite boulders, Silver Falls crashes down a cliff so steep that you can nose the bow of your boat under the falling water, and Spray of Pearls Falls, as delicate as its name, is all mist and rainbows in a mossy canyon.

Indian Arm has long been a favourite rendezvous with boaters, and no wonder. Ruggedly scenic, but protected enough even for small boats, and deep and clear enough for large ones. An area simple to navigate.

A fascinating approach, past the docks and loading cranes of Vancouver Harbour, and under the Second Narrows Bridge. A little farther, a turn, and you're within the green solitude of Indian Arm. Surprising to find such a secluded fiord, such undeveloped shoreline, so close to the highrises of a major city.

Endless possibilities of exploration. So much to do. So many places to stop awhile. At Belcarra Park the lawns and beach and shade trees make this a good spot for children — room for running, and jigging for fish and crabs from the wharf.

At Deep Cove, a motley group of little ships at anchor, an interesting collection of "things" afloat. The town is an easy stop for forgotten supplies, and the marina the only fuel source in the Arm.

Farther up the Arm, summer cottages cluster where the ground is level. Quarries and logging camps. Islands and forest and waterfalls and steep-sided mountains. The Buntzen Lake Power Plant,[8] a strangely ornate building for a site so stark. An Indian rock painting nearby. A magnificent pair of swans behind Croker Island,[9] near an abandoned landing. At Granite Falls, a picnic site. And good fishing at the mouth of Indian River.

The best-known site of all is Wigwam Inn, a grand dilapidated derelict of a building. Wander over the grounds to see what once the rich and racy came to enjoy: the walks and rockeries, the gardens and gazebo, and the seaside swimming pool.

Go up — about a ten-minute walk — to where Cathedral Canyon comes abruptly and splendidly to an end. The trail stops without warning at the edge of a precipice. Look down — if you dare — to the creek below, and then look up to the most sensational waterfall in Indian Arm: Spray of Pearls Falls.

Did you know: A local diver, Duane Goertson, discovered a new species of chiton in Indian Arm. The chiton has been named *Tonicella goertsoni*.

Spray of Pearls Falls

Bridge, and lagoon outflow into Deep Bay

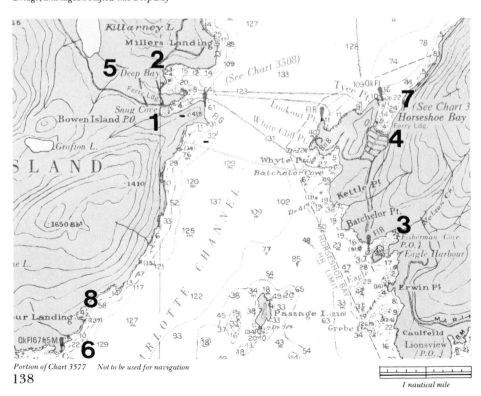

Portion of Chart 3577   Not to be used for navigation

1 nautical mile

31

Queen Charlotte Channel

What's There nostalgia — the ruins of a large excursion resort....sandy beach in Deep Bay....fishing....a walk between lagoon and lake....almost-tame ducks to feed....

Charts
3508 large scale plans of Snug Cove and Deep Bay   1:8000
3586 Howe Sound   1:37,500

Moorage In Snug Cove,[1] a public wharf and anchorage, but be warned: this is the most popular cruising stop in Howe Sound
   The car ferry docks with a great deal of noise and turbulence next to the floats
   In Deep Bay,[2] anchorage open to the wash from passing ferries

Facilities At Snug Cove, groceries, cafe, and limited marina services
   Across the channel at Fishermans Cove[3] and at Horseshoe Bay,[4] complete marina and repair services. Horseshoe Bay, a very busy ferry terminal, also offers a variety of stores and restaurants, a neighbourhood pub, boat rentals, and bus service to Vancouver

Caution Queen Charlotte Channel is a heavy traffic area, a thoroughfare for freighters, ferries, tugs, and fleets of sailboats. Be careful at night when navigation lights are difficult to see against the background of shore lights. And watch for booms and barges towed behind tugs: never try to pass between them.

Access By boat, or by car ferry from Horseshoe Bay
   Launching ramps: Fishermans Cove; Horseshoe Bay

Snug Cove is the nearest island retreat for Lower Mainland boaters, often a first night moorage during a weekend cruise in Howe Sound, and a popular stop for small boats launched at Horseshoe Bay for a day of fishing. On a sunny summer day "The Cove" is a festival of boats and ferry-loads of people, much as it might have been in the heyday of steamship excursions and evening "booze cruises". Then holidayers came to the nine hundred acres of groomed parkland of Bowen Estates, to the riding trails and picnic lawns and dance pavillion. Now the resort is in ruins, but traces of it make for interesting exploring: wander over the grounds and cross the little bridge by the lagoon to stretch boat-cramped legs.

Find the foundations of the old hotel at Deep Bay, still known as Hotel Bay by some, and nearby, the swimming pool, tennis courts and lawn bowling green, all in disrepair. The orchard trees and formal gardens are wild and weathered; rusty lamp posts and crumbling rock walls mark the promenade around the lagoon. The pink sand imported to cover the shoreline of Deep Bay has washed away, but the stretch of native gray sand is still a popular beach.

Always cool and shady, the walk to Bridal Falls on Killarney Creek[5] crosses a network of lanes through a stand of evergreens between the Snug Cove Road and the creek itself. Old cabins crouching in the gloom beside the lanes are collapsing under the weight of moss and years. The falls aren't visible from the trail, but you can hear them and scramble down the path to them.

The main trail follows the creek right up to Killarney Lake, joining the paved road up to the Catholic church and dipping into the woods again, edging the fallow fields of the old resort farm. Look for deer feeding in the clearings, and for the herd of horses running wild over the island. Turning left at the lake, the dirt road joins pavement again: about twenty minutes of walking back to Snug Cove.

Queen Charlotte Channel offers miles of shoreline to explore and shelter enough in a choice of coves. And for fishermen, some of the most productive fishing in Howe Sound. Try Cowans Point[6] at the south end of Bowen Island, "Hole in the Wall" near Horseshoe Bay,[7] or "the Coppermine",[8] about half a mile north of Cowans and with Seymour Landing handy as a picnic site.

If, when fishing here, you hear the surprising sound of a steam whistle, look across the channel to see the Royal Hudson chuffing her daily summer run to Squamish, and dragging skirts of steam along the British Columbia Railway above Howe Sound.

Did you know: Lord Louis Mountbatten of Burma is a member of the Bowen Island Legion.

"A simple plan...we head for a nice quiet spot where the winner was caught in past years."

Norris – The Vancouver Sun

A midsummer attraction, and a midsummer madness: the Sun Free Salmon Derby, in which conglomerations of fisherpeople cover the derby area shore-to-shore with boats, trying to bag one of ten prize-winning fish.

On Thornbrough's safe, calm, waters

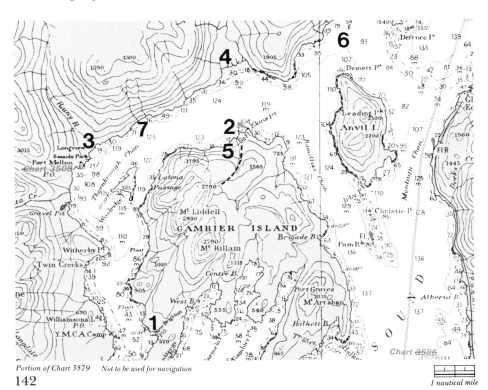

1 nautical mile

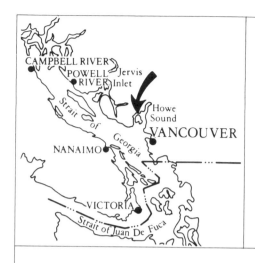

32

Thornbrough Channel

What's There secluded picnic spots....a climb to a trout-filled lake....salmon fishing....calm water....a pulp mill and undeveloped shores....log booms....crabs....Indian pictograph....

Charts

3586 Howe Sound   1:37,500

Moorage At New Brighton,[1] public floats fairly open to boat wash and waves

Limited anchorage because of very deep water in the channel; a boat or two could anchor beside the Thunderbird Yacht Club floats at Ekins Point Landing [2]

Boats commonly moor against the log booms in the channel

Facilities None, in northern Thornbrough Channel

At Port Mellon,[3] telephone service and road connection to Gibsons, an hotel and cafe for mill workers

At Hopkins Landing near the Langdale Ferry Terminal, a small general store by a public wharf

Nearest marina services at Gibsons

Caution Never tie your boat on the shore side of a boom or even into a space between logs because logs are shifting, restless things and booms can move to force a boat against the shore. And never try walking across the logs: that is trespassing, but more to the point, it is dangerous.

Access Road to Port Mellon, but by boat only to most parts of Thornbrough Channel

Launching ramp: Gibsons

At New Brighton, a few homes; at McNab Creek,[4] a busy logging camp and a defunct recreation development; at Seaside Park,[3] beside the Rainy River, a company community for pulp mill employees; and at Laytona Beach[5] and Potlatch Creek,[6] youth camps — but the rest of Thornbrough Channel is forest and cliff and deep deep water, and a feeling of isolation that belies the fact that Vancouver is less than twenty miles away.

Thornbrough is very much the loggers' channel, with skid roads and boom-boats, log dumps and spar trees, and Port Mellon, the oldest pulp mill in B.C. A possible find: an iron shoe from oxen teams used to log the slopes along the channel. Drop into the museum at nearby Gibsons to see such logging relics.

An abandoned log dump can also be a museum of sorts: a mass of litter and leavings make it a bonanza for scroungers. In one such dump east of Stolterfoht Creek[7] bits of machinery stick through gravel like old bones not properly buried.

This landing is ideal for beach parties, with its shade trees, wild flowers, berry bushes, stream, and a cleared area safe for campfires. A trail through the bush joins the stream at a log bridge. Above the bridge the water has cut out a small canyon with falls and pools that are marvellously cool and clear.

During summer the icy-cold fresh waters of the flooding Squamish River extend down the main channel of Howe Sound, and make finding water warm enough for swimming a problem. But along the "backwash" of the north shore of Thornbrough Channel the water near some of the pocket-size gravel beaches is comfortable enough. In 1792 Captain Vancouver noticed the drama-tic difference in these waters: "the colour of the water changed from being nearly milk white, and almost fresh, to that of oceanic and perfectly salt." And, he might have added, from "cold" to "not so cold".

The waters off McNab Creek are favoured fishing territory. Pleasant to drift here, even when the fish aren't biting. The valley above the creek, wide and gently rounded, scooped and smoothed by ancient glaciers into the "U"-shape of a dugout canoe. Look along the cliff east of the creek for an Indian pictograph, quite small and difficult to find.

Across the channel, the floats at Ekins Point Landing mark the beginning of a trail — a very invigorating climb — to a trout lake high on Gambier Island. An hour of tramping up, and less to scramble down.

Did you know: Port Mellon is the oldest pulp mill in the province.

Rainy Day Survival

The northwest climate being what it is, every boat, but especially those with children aboard, needs a wet-weather survival kit. The most important part of the kit is invisible: the attitude that a rainy day, even on a boat, can be fun.

Play games. The old standbys, checkers and chess, take little space. A deck of cards takes even less space. Take a pocket book of card game rules. Many new games on the market appeal to children and adults alike, and come in compact boxes: browse past the games department and stock up.

Read. Many marinas and shoreside stores feature book-trade shelves: you leave a pocketbook or two for every one you take. A constant change of reading material, but without the build-up of damp books on your boat.

Cultivate hobbies. Those that travel well. Play a harmonica. Knit a toque for everyone aboard. Practise complicated knots. Whittle driftwood.

Swim. In the rain, when water seems even warmer, it's good exercise that doesn't wet your clothes.

Re-design the interior of your boat. Re-design the boat.

Take a long walk, to that trout lake on Gambier, for instance; sitting around all day lowers crew morale. Go just before bedtime: everyone will sleep better, and clothing will have a chance to dry overnight.

Make a long passage. The water on rainy days is often dead calm. A new landfall adds sparkle to an otherwise dull day.

Keep clothing as dry as possible. Lacking rain gear, cut holes for head and arms in large plastic bags to make effective ponchos. Without rubber boots you can keep feet comparatively dry by wearing plastic sandwich bags between stocking feet and deck shoes. Remember that with dry head and feet, the rest of the body feels warmer.

Take all the damp clothing and bedding to the nearest laundromat, with a deck of cards and a picnic lunch. Start a laundromat party.

Plan a cruise to the sunny south.

"The Beachcombers" film set, near Gibsons wharf

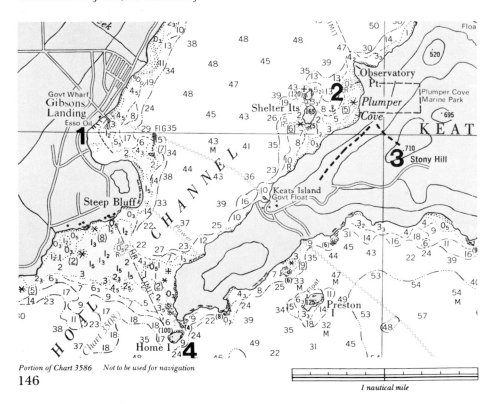

Portion of Chart 3586   Not to be used for navigation

1 nautical mile

33

Plumper Cove Marine Park and Gibsons Landing

What's There marine park....wilderness walks....mountaintop view....fishing....museum...."The Beachcombers" filming location....

Charts
3508 Shoal Channel large scale plans   1:12,000
3586 Howe Sound   1:37,500

Moorage At Gibsons,[1] a public wharf behind a breakwater
  At Plumper Cove,[2] good anchorage and landing floats for small craft

Facilities Plumper Cove Marine Park: 78 acres, picnic and camp sites, water taps, pit toilets, field with fruit trees, trails
  Gibsons: marina services and a variety of retail stores; charts

Caution Watch for the sunken rock south of the Plumper Cove wharf: occasionally an anchored boat is grounded at low tide.

Access By boat only to Plumper Cove Marine Park; water taxi available at Gibsons
  Car ferry from Horseshoe Bay to Langdale, and road to Gibsons
  Launching ramp: Gibsons

Plumper Cove Marine Park is close to Vancouver, is in the protected cruising waters of Howe Sound, and is close to some of the best fishing around. The park would be popular even if it were not also very lovely. The park covers seventy-eight acres, some developed, some left natural. Gravel beaches for driftwood fires. Campsites and picnic tables that command waterfront views. A grass playing field equally irresistible to deer and to children. A few apple trees, the remains of a farm orchard. In the fall pick tart apples, and in summer sit in apple-tree shade. The rest of the park, covered with lush stands of timber with little undergrowth: walk freely in a field of giant trunks. Observatory Point, a grandstand for sunsets. And the hike to the top of Stony Hill,[3] for an eagle's view of islands and passages, and across the Strait of Georgia to Vancouver Island.

Join the ever-hopeful fishing crowds at Gower Point and at Home Island,[4] locally called "Salmon Rock". Divers find treasure-hauls of fishing gear along the Shoal, the lip being a real tackle-grabber. Forty fathoms of water, and then suddenly two.

The mainland shore of Shoal Channel is a cliff as stark and steep as a castle wall, and was once a place of Indian sentries watching for raiding parties that came from the north. Behind the cliff lies Gibsons Landing — now just "Gibsons"; we're on a first-name basis. This town has a split personality. The old section, sprawling around wharf and waterfront, was the landing for home-steaders and loggers, and now for fishboats and cruising people. The new part of the town turns its back on all of that: it's built farther up the hill, courting the road-bound people. Up here the liquor store and shopping centre, tucked away like candy on a high shelf. Hike up the hill, but the walk is steep and the taxi service at the bottom is a temptation hardly worth resisting. Except when blackberries are ripe along the road.

Did you know: The C.B.C. television series "The Beachcomers" is filmed on location at Gibsons. Look for "Nick", and "Relic", and the *Persephone* near Molly's Reach.

Cruising Metric

Canadian measurements will officially be converted to the Metric System by the early 1980s. Some metric charts are already available, and metric units are now used in weather reports.

Length and Distance:

Though kilometres replace statute miles, the nautical mile, representing one minute of latitude on the earth's surface, continues to be a basic nautical measure of distance:

    1 nautical mile = 1.15 statute mile
    1 nautical mile = 1852 metres or 6080 feet
    1 cable   = 0.10 nautical mile
    1 knot   = 1 nautical mile per hour

A fathom is equal to six feet, but depths on the metric charts will be in metres:

    1 metre   = 39.37 inches
    1 foot   = 0.305 metres
    1 fathom = 1.829 metres

Atmospheric Pressure: 1 kilopascal = 1.295 inches mercury

    98 kPa = 28.94 inches mercury
    99 kPa = 29.24 inches mercury
  100 kPa = 29.53 inches mercury
  101 kPa = 29.83 inches mercury
  102 kPa = 30.12 inches mercury
  103 kPa = 30.42 inches mercury

More important than the actual reading of pressure on the barometer is any indication of change in atmospheric pressure. Rising? Fair weather ahead. Falling? Worse weather to come. Holding steady? Whatever the weather, expect more of the same. Generally the faster the change of pressure, the faster and the more extreme will be the change in weather.

Temperature:

1° Celsius = 1.8° Fahrenheit

°C	°F	Comments
-10	14	icy, cold day
-5	23	brisk
0	32	water freezes
5	41	chilly day
10	50	wear a sweater
15	59	cool day
20	68	room temperature
25	77	pleasantly warm
30	86	hot day
35	95	tepid water
40	104	sweltering day

Wind Warnings:

17 - 33 knots: small craft warning
Sea: whitecaps, some spray
34 - 47 knots: gale warning
Sea: breaking crests, blowing foam
Over 48 knots: storm warning
Sea: very large waves, driving spray

Rainfall: measured in millimetres
1 mm = 0.039 inch

Capacity:

    1 American gal. = 0.80 Imperial gal.
    1 litre   = 0.220 Imperial gal.
    1 Imperial gal. = 4.546 litre
    1 American gal. = 3.785 litre

Chapter Five
Upper Strait of Georgia

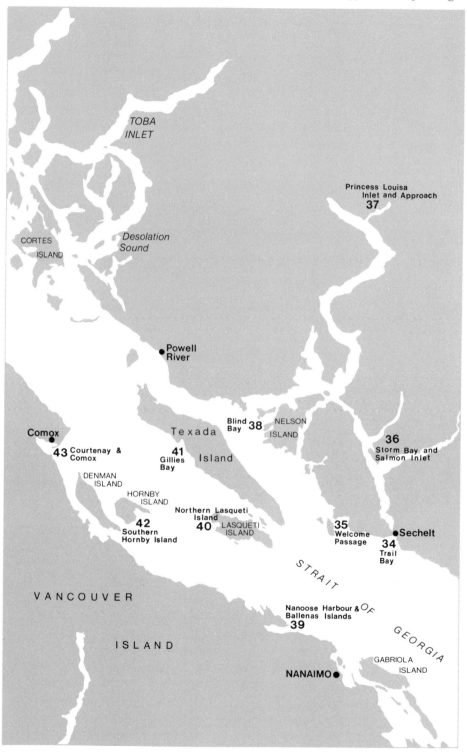

TOBA
INLET

Princess Louisa
Inlet and Approach
37

CORTES
ISLAND

*Desolation
Sound*

● Powell
River

Comox
● **43** Courtenay &
Comox

Texada

Blind
Bay **38**

NELSON
ISLAND

36
Storm Bay and
Salmon Inlet

41
Gillies
Bay

Island

DENMAN
ISLAND

HORNBY
ISLAND

Northern Lasqueti
Island
40

LASQUETI
ISLAND

35
Welcome
Passage

●Sechelt
34
Trail
Bay

42
Southern
Hornby Island

STRAIT

OF

VANCOUVER

Nanoose Harbour &
Ballenas Islands
39

GEORGIA

ISLAND

GABRIOLA
ISLAND

NANAIMO ●

Protected anchorage in Trail Bay, near Sechelt

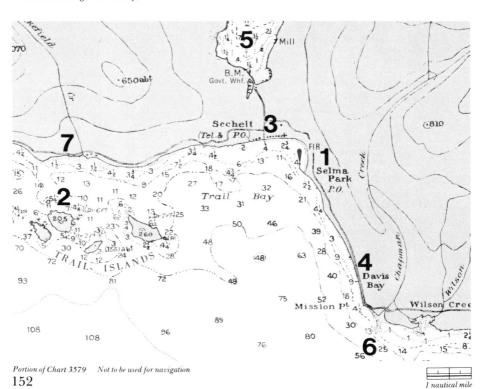

Portion of Chart 3579   Not to be used for navigation

1 nautical mile

34

Trail Bay

What's There beachcombing....waterfront pub....crabs....good emergency anchorage....wild berries....fishing....village shopping....beachside municipal picnic park....

Charts

3577 Sand Heads to Ballenas Islands   1:77,300

Moorage No public wharf in the bay; at Selma Park,[1] good anchorage behind a rock breakwater

In the lee of the Trail Islands,[2] the last chance for shelter during the 18-mile haul from Welcome Passage to Howe Sound

Facilities At Sechelt,[3] groceries, hardware, banks, liquor store, laundromat, various specialty stores, and medical services

At Davis Bay,[4] motels, restaurant, grocery store near the beach; a wharf in poor condition used by tug boats

On Porpoise Bay,[5] boating facilities — only half a mile from Trail Bay by land but over 50 miles away by water! Nearest marina services on the Strait side, at Secret Cove

Caution Entering Trail Bay from the east, give Mission Point[6] a wide berth: a sand bar extends seaward about a quarter of a mile.

Access Car access along Trail Bay

No launching ramps in Trail Bay; nearest ramps at Halfmoon Bay, to the west

Trail Bay boasts the simplest ingredients to pleasant boating: clear waters, good fishing, and a sheltered place to drop anchor for the night. A perfect spot for those who like their cruising quiet and low-key.

An elegant curve of gravel from point to point, the beach is marvellous. Mile after mile of stone and gravel, with tide marks of tangled kelp, and driftwood in fantastic shapes. Swimming, fine when the incoming tide is warmed and covers the barnacled lower reaches of the beach. On shore by the breakwater at Selma Park, pockets of fine sand keep children busy for hours. Sometimes the resident platoon of snow geese marches along the shore or paddles to the boats for handouts.

Following the shore past the breakwater anchorage, a dirt road separates tall blackberry hedges and passes through the Indian Reserve. Skiffs and floats and fishing nets piled along the beach. Farther on, a small municipal park with picnic tables. And Teredo Street, apt name in a town between two salt-water bays.

Tugboaters will not risk a boom breaking up in choppy seas: tugs nursing their booms in the lee of the Trail Islands are useful indicators of wave conditions out in the Strait of Georgia, for boats lacking up-to-date weather reports. As long as the tugboaters keep the logs in shelter, you know the passage is bound to be rough.

A visit to Wakefield Inn[7] can ease the tedium of waiting out a storm. After the two-mile hike from the breakwater moorage, you'll feel you deserve a drink in the friendly old pub with its grand view over the Strait. But when the weather is calm and the sun is over the yard-arm, anchor outside the Wakefield and row ashore. Sunset over Vancouver Island is spectacular enough, but even more spectacular with the silhouette of your own boat against the fiery sky.

Did you know: Many years ago a marine railway crossed the half–mile of land between Trail Bay and Porpoise Bay, saving boats the fifty-mile voyage around the Sechelt Peninsula.

Anchoring

When moorage is crowded, noisy and expensive, the alternative is to anchor. A securely anchored boat has all the sea for a moat around it, and a dinghy for a drawbridge. And all you need is some simple gear, a suitable place, and a bit of know-how.

Ground tackle:

Anchor suitable to the size of the boat.

Anchor line non-floating, and long enough and strong enough for your boat. For a boat up to 8 metres (26 feet), 61 metres (200 feet) of 12.7 mm (½ inch) line is generally sufficient.

Chain about 6 metres (20 feet) shackled between the anchor and the line prevents chafing of the line against rocks, and the weight of the chain helps the anchor to dig in.

Anchorage:

Is there enough protection from wind and waves, even if the wind changes direction?

Will there be enough water under the keel at low tide?

Is there enough room for your boat to swing without hitting shore, shoals, or other boats? Remember that if you anchor at high tide your boat will swing farther at low water.

What kind of holding ground does the anchorage have? Mud, sand, and gravel are usually best; rock is poor, and kelp can tangle in the anchor flukes. Symbols on the chart tell you what to expect.

Setting an anchor:

Stop your boat where you want the anchor set.

Lower the anchor slowly while counting off how much line is needed to touch the bottom.

Run the boat astern slowly, paying out the anchor line until you have enough scope for safety. Scope is the ratio between length of rode (anchor line) and depth of water from chocks to bottom. A scope of 3:1 means that in 3 metres (10 feet) of water you have let out 9 metres (30 feet) of rode. More scope — 7:1 — increases the holding power of the anchor.

Snub the line: you should feel the anchor drag, catch, hold, and stop the boat.

Fasten the line to a cleat and shut off the engine. You are anchored.

For small boats and for large ones, calm moorage in Smuggler Cove

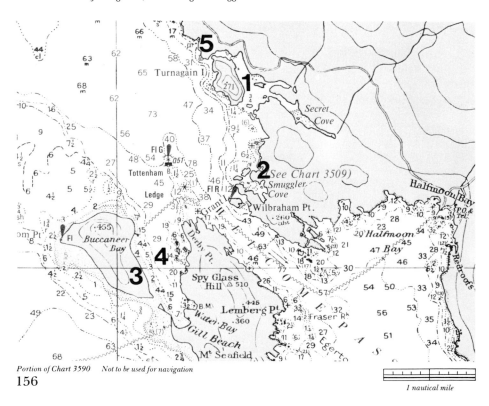

Portion of Chart 3590   Not to be used for navigation

156

1 nautical mile

35

Welcome Passage

What's There sandy beaches and hidden coves....small-boat camping....undeveloped marine park....formal dining at a nearby resort....salmon fishing year round....crabbing....

Charts

3509 Welcome Passage large scale plans	1:24,300
3577 Sand Heads to Ballenas Islands	1:77,300

Moorage At Secret Cove,[1] all-weather anchorage and moorage at public floats and marina slips

In Smuggler Cove,[2] no public landing dock, but anchorage

At Thormanby Islands, a public float for day use at Veaucroft Beach,[3] and fair-weather anchorage in Buccaneer Bay[4]

Facilities At Secret Cove, marina services and general store; showers, laundry, charts, charters; transportation available to Lord Jim's Lodge at nearby Oles Cove

Smuggler Cove Marine Park, undeveloped; no drinking water

At Thormanby Islands, no facilities

Caution Entrance to Secret Cove is to the left of the red conical buoy which marks a rock drying at a 12-foot tide.

In Buccaneer Bay be aware of a steep drop-off near the beach between the islands; do not anchor near the drop-off.

Access Car access to Secret Cove; by boat only to Smuggler Cove and to Thormanby Islands

Launching ramp: Secret Cove

Welcome Passage is within easy weekend reach of Vancouver and makes a popular shakedown cruise. It is also a popular stop on the way to Desolation Sound. Why this popularity? Variety. From eagle eyries to formal restaurant; marinas in one cove and marine park in another; rocky islets and sand beaches.

Variety even in the fishing. Try for coho, lingcod and flatfish at Epsom Point; for bluebacks and rockfish at Tottenham Ledge; and through Welcome Passage troll for whatever takes the bait. A winter run of chinook right into Secret Cove — a comfortably calm spot in which to put down a line when the winds are blowing.

A word about mooring in Secret Cove: when anchoring, choose a spot well out of the way of traffic, burn a mooring light, and during the cruise season be prepared for a constant wash from passing boats. The public floats are usually crowded, and you will have to raft up. A courtesy: ask permission, bumper well, and tie your mooring lines to the dock rather than to the other boat so that his lines need not carry the strain of both boats. Remember that workboats and fishermen often want to leave in the very early hours of the morning, and will move any boats rafted outside them. Trifling problems, these, against the fact that Secret Cove offers such security, and so many amenities.

On Thormanby Island, sand to sift, sand to sit on, sand to work between your toes. Hot summer day beaches here are glorious, and the water so clear that you can drift shoreward and not tell by looking down whether the sand bottom is one, or ten metres below until your keel nudges bottom. Set a crab net before coming closer in to anchor.

If you tire of sand, an altogether different face of the Thormanby Islands looks to the open Strait. A wild and lonely face. Walk over a jumble of boulders under steep escarpments.

As different again, and just as intriguing, is Smuggler Cove with its half-hidden entrance tricky to negotiate, but with a passage deep enough and clear enough to admit most cruising boats. The undeveloped marine park, enclosing the entire cove and all but one of the islands in the entrance, offers simply a bluff to clamber over, what's left of logging roads to explore, and water summer-warmed to swim in. And the adventure of following a trail that joins Secret Cove and Smuggler Cove: wonderful names!

Did you know: Most of the place names near Welcome Passage originate with a horse race in England, the 1860 Derby. Buccaneer Bay has nothing to do with pirates: Buccaneer was a favourite in the race; the winner was Thormanby, his owner, Mr. Merry. The outcome of the race was Welcome news — for those who bet on the winners.

White sand beaches and heaps of driftwood at Thormanby Islands

1 nautical mile

36

Storm Bay and Salmon Inlet

What's There a twelve-mile-long fiord....pictographs....magnificent scenery....secluded gravel beaches....excellent fishing....Clowhom Lake Hydro Dam....lake swimming and lake-trout fishing....

Charts

3589 Jervis Inlet and Approaches   1:76,400

Moorage In Storm Bay,[1] anchorage behind two islets at the mouth, or in the bay itself, on mud bottom

In Salmon Inlet, anchorage in the cove past Misery Creek,[2] where a logging camp stores its log booms

With permission, temporary moorage at Weldwood Company floats at the head of Salmon Inlet[3]

Facilities None, in Storm Bay or Salmon Inlet

Nearest marina services and general cruising supplies at Egmont or at Porpoise Bay

Caution "Skookumchuck" means "strong water": the rapids in the narrows reach 12 knots and can be heard for miles when running full. Take these rapids at slack current. Check at the Egmont Store if in doubt about the timing.

Access By boat only, to Storm Bay and to Salmon Inlet

Launching ramps: Egmont; Porpoise Bay

Backed against the strong winds from the south, Storm Bay is a secure anchorage which couldn't be more conveniently placed: within easy reach of any part of the branching inlets. Perfect.

At the entrance to the bay on the rocky south shore, a tame and gentle anchorage with a cabin in the open and goats wandering about. Inside the bay, the few cabins are scarcely noticed because of the trees: nothing ruins the wild grandeur of Storm Bay. It's a space hollowed out of a rain-forest coastline, out of an evergreen jungle. The edges of everything blurred by a green shagginess; logs and tideline rocks slippery with moss; and even the eelgrass shaggy, growing in vast underwater fields spooky to row across.

The west side of Sechelt Inlet leans back against the Caren Range, an unpretentious set of hills when compared to the cliffs and peaks across the channel. Be a connoisseur of beaches on this gentle shore: pick and choose from wide gravel sweeps, or small pockets of gravel bracketed between stone outcrops, or fans of delta silt where the creeks empty. The water is brisk for swimming: better to build a driftwood fire, season permitting. Or explore trails that disappear into mountain alder.

The view up Salmon Inlet pulls at you: twelve miles of magnificent mountains. Go past Chum Point, and Steelhead Point. What's in a name? Good salmon fishing, from the sound of it. But any way, Salmon Inlet is spectacular: Misery Creek Falls, a dazzling slash of water; a hydro dam; and pictographs.

At an intriguing rock painting on the north shore less than two miles from the head of the inlet, pull your boat right up against the cliff and step off onto a narrow ledge where the artist must have stood to paint the single file of plodding deer and the sinister little two-headed serpent coiled around another deer. You can see where the artist spilled some stain into a crevice in the rock. How long ago?

At the head of the inlet, a Weldwood logging camp, and the Clowhom Lake Hydro Dam. The chart says "waterfall", but it is canned and controlled when pushing turbines. There's a waterfall only when the spillway is open. Ask permission to land at the Weldwood wharf; the men will give directions to the trail that leads to a beach at Clowhom Lake. Good swimming here, and good trout fishing too.

Did you know: Rubbing lemon juice on your hands after cleaning fish will help get rid of the fishy odour on your skin.

Salmon Chowder

    ½ cup melted butter
    1 cup chopped celery
    1 cup chopped onion
    2 cups chopped new potatoes (raw)
    ½ cup flour
    ¼ teaspoon pepper
    ½ teaspoon salt
    5 cups milk
    1 can (6 ounces) evaporated milk
    2 cups salmon (1 pound cooked)

Melt butter in large heavy pot, then sauté celery, onion, and potatoes together for 20 minutes, stirring often. Stir in flour, pepper, and salt until blended, then slowly add milk and evaporated milk. Stir until mixture thickens. Add flaked salmon, and serve just before mixture boils.

Serves 4 to 6.

Daphne Hale

from *Vancouver Aquarium Seafood Recipes*

Facing Salmon Inlet

Looking down Chatterbox Falls

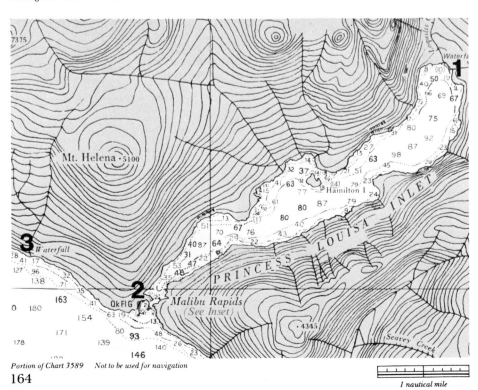

Portion of Chart 3589   Not to be used for navigation

1 nautical mile

37

Princess Louisa Inlet and Approach

What's There the most spectacular mountain scenery on the coast....marine park....Malibu Rapids....waterfalls....fishing....shellfish....summer swimming....pictographs....

Charts

3589 Jervis Inlet and Approaches	1:76,400
with insets of Princess Louisa Inlet	1:36,700
inset of Malibu Rapids	1:12,200

Moorage At Princess Louisa Marine Park,[1] public floats and anchorage nearby, where depths permit

At Malibu Club,[2] temporary visitors' moorage

Facilities Princess Louisa Marine Park: 40 acres, picnic tables, pit toilets, drinking water, rain shelter; park rangers during the cruise season

Malibu Club, a camp for young people, allows visitors a brief tour of the camp; snack bar and "trading post"

Nearest fuel, store and telephone at Egmont, 32 miles from Malibu Rapids

Caution Currents through the very narrow Malibu Rapids reach 9 knots. Go through when the current is near slack. Watch for other boats.

Access By boat only

Nearest launching ramps: Saltery Bay; Egmont

At the very head of Princess Louisa Inlet, surrounding 120-foot-high Chatterbox Falls,[1] is a provincial government Class A marine park that is the legacy of James F. Macdonald, who lived here much of his life and left the unique property to public trust. An act of generosity appreciated by the hundreds of people who come here every year.

The approach up Jervis Inlet to Princess Louisa Inlet is a scenic tour on a splendid scale. Each mile bringing the mountains closer in. The peaks reaching for snow, and keeping it all year round. The cliffs, like icebergs, showing only their upper parts, and on a calm day standing doubly tall on their reflections.

Look for pictographs on patches of light-coloured granite, usually on steep cliffs above deep water. The Indian paintings often mark a location of particular power and significance: a current pass, a prominent vantage point, a year-round stream. No lack of such in Jervis Inlet!

While waiting for slack current for passage through Malibu Rapids, look for a spectacular waterfall[3] on the eastern shore of Queens Reach, not far past Malibu Club. Moor against a steep-sided rock by the falls. The adventurous-minded can climb into a niche behind the falling water, into a frightening, exhilarating shower of numbing noise and stinging spray.

Captain Vancouver looked for anchorage at Malibu Rapids in 1792, but the current was flowing outward, and thinking the outflow to be a mountain river he never guessed at the inlet beyond.

Princess Louisa Inlet, only four miles long and not a mile at its widest, is an exhibition of mountains, a pageant of cliffs, an extravaganza of waterfalls. Cliffs running water in vertical sheets. Streams tumbling over concave rock faces and falling free for hundreds of feet before striking rock again. Swim in the shadow of a glacier. Fish for salmon in a salt-water mountain "lake". Or simply anchor near the "chattering" roar of Chatterbox Falls.

Did you know: Some soundings in Jervis Inlet approach 400 fathoms — much deeper than anywhere else in the Strait of Georgia.

Provincial Marine Parks in the Upper Strait of Georgia

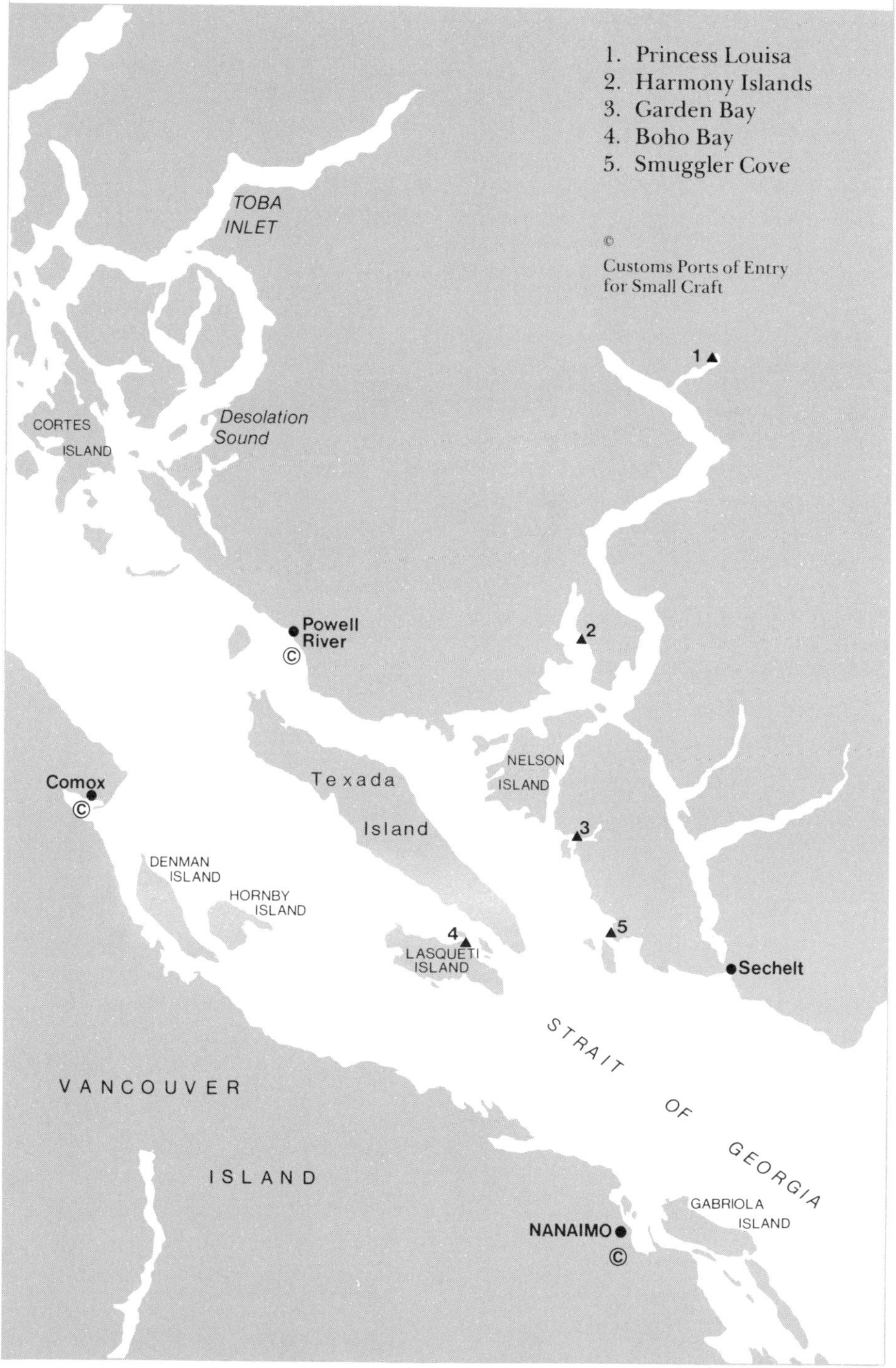

1. Princess Louisa
2. Harmony Islands
3. Garden Bay
4. Boho Bay
5. Smuggler Cove

©

Customs Ports of Entry
for Small Craft

*TOBA
INLET*

*Desolation
Sound*

CORTES
ISLAND

1 ▲

● Powell
River
©

▲ 2

NELSON
ISLAND

Comox
©

T e x a d a

Island

▲ 3

DENMAN
ISLAND

HORNBY
ISLAND

4 ▲
LASQUETI
ISLAND

▲ 5

● Sechelt

V A N C O U V E R

S T R A I T

O F

G E O R G I A

I S L A N D

GABRIOLA
ISLAND

NANAIMO ●
©

167

Moss-covered banks above Blind Bay

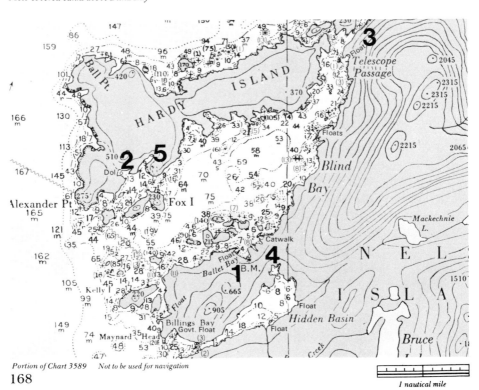

Portion of Chart 3589   Not to be used for navigation

1 nautical mile

38

Blind Bay

What's There oysters....squirrels....forest trails....pleasant anchorages....a miniature fiord....bluff covered in deep, deep moss....

Charts

3589 Jervis Inlet and Approaches   1:76,400

Moorage In Blind Bay, no public wharves

Good anchorage in Ballet Bay[1] and behind Fox Island;[2] sometimes log booms to raft against

Facilities In Blind Bay, none

Near the ferry slip at Saltery Bay, a public wharf, a small grocery store, and restaurant with lounge

Nearest complete marina services at Pender Harbour, within 10 miles of Blind Bay; and at Egmont, fuel, groceries, showers and laundry, some hardware and accommodation

Caution Watch for shoals and drying rocks throughout Blind Bay, and for a mid-channel rock in Telescope Passage.[3]

Access By boat only

Launching ramps: Saltery Bay; Egmont

Some places seem to hold on to light even on a gloomy day. Blind Bay, for instance. Protected, but not hemmed in: a good place to wait for better weather before heading up Jervis Inlet, where the narrow channels hold on to the clouds. And with Telescope Passage to let you conveniently out the "top" end, Blind Bay does double duty as a delightful cruising stop and as a calm and open approach to Jervis.

Islands and coves galore! A marvellous choice of anchorages! Moor in a spot apart, or find the company of others. Blind Bay is large enough to absorb a lot of boats and still seem pleasantly secluded.

What's there to do? There's a trail between Ballet Bay and Hidden Basin:[4] about a mile to walk. And perfect picnic sites, islets covered with grass and moss and wild flowers, and perhaps a dwarf tree or two, and with shoreline of smooth granite that seems somehow to be softer than sand. The water is warm enough for swimming in summer. Or try for salmon around the entrance of the bay, and down the Nelson Island coastline. Or drop a codline somewhere near Telescope Passage: perhaps you'll tie into a red snapper, surely the finest food fish to be had.

There's an incredibly beautiful spot by a small inlet[5] on the Hardy Island shore, opposite Fox Island. The inlet itself is unique: narrow, steep-sided and surprisingly deep, a fiord in perfect miniature. It curves so that when you anchor near its head, rock walls surround you. Once anchored, you feel that everything else is shut out, and your attention turns inward.

At the end of the inlet a curved granite shelf makes a natural dinghy landing above an oyster bed. The shore is barred by giant firs and cedars. Past these, a muted, muffled forest. A wonderland, hardly real. Evergreen-filtered light falls like rain into soft sun splotches. The towering trees hold silent spaces between them. You find yourself whispering.

A natural path follows the slope between rock ridges. The magic increases with every step. At first the footing is soft and spongy. Higher up the footing is softer still — there's moss on everything. Deep, deep moss. It blurs the edge of things, takes their shapes away. Rocks turned to formless mounds; and logs, green amorphous heaps. The ridge tops are level and deeply and greenly carpeted with moss. Stretch out on it. Luxuriously. Stay awhile, and very still, and soon the squirrels approach. Either so tame or so wild that they have no fear of people.

An altogether enchanted place.

Did you know: The eulachon, or candlefish, is so rich in oil that Indians dried them, fitted them with wicks of cedar fibre, and used them as candles.

Easy Oysters

An oyster's only defence is a stoic resistance, a tight-lipped opposition to being pried apart. Shucking an oyster can be a gruesome operation, with all the blood coming from the operator. But it isn't necessary. Let the shell become the pan in which the oyster stews in its own juice: steam it.

First, scrub the shells thoroughly, or they'll smell while cooking. Most important, *keep the round side of the oyster shell underneath*. And keep the oysters level or the liquid will seep out and then they won't steam — They'll Petrify.

In an ordinary pan: Place a handful of pebbles in a large heavy frying pan and add boiling water to the top of the pebbles. Place oysters, round side down, on the pebbles. Cover the pan with a lid or foil. Simmer for about 5 to 10 minutes, or until the oysters are done.

On a barbecue or hibachi: Place the scrubbed oysters, round side down, on the grill about 100 mm (4 inches) above the hot coals. This method will take a little longer: about 15 minutes.

In a campfire: Wrap the scrubbed oysters in double thickness of foil and place them, round side down, among the hot coals at the edge of the fire. Check them after about 10 minutes.

In an oven: Wrap each well-scrubbed oyster in foil and place, round side down, in a moderately hot oven (180°C or 350°F) for about 10 to 15 minutes.

Note: Steaming time depends on the size of the oysters. Best to check after 5 minutes. The shells will open only a fraction of an inch, and some won't open at all without a little prising, but that's still easier than shucking.

Oyster toppings: When the oysters are done, remove the top shells and serve them in their bottom shells, sprinkled with one of these toppings: lemon juice, lemon pepper, sweet pepper flakes, grated cheese, melted butter, curry powder, barbecue sauce, ketchup, or .... try a combination.

Submarine in Nanoose Harbour

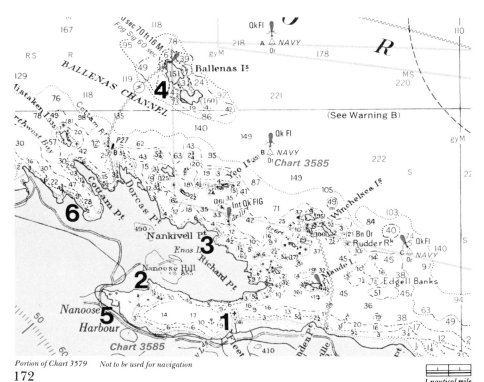

Portion of Chart 3579   Not to be used for navigation

1 nautical mile

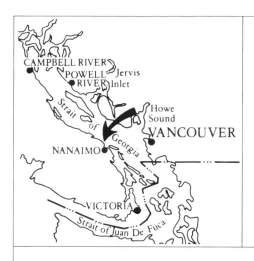

39

Nanoose Harbour and Ballenas Islands

What's There salmon and submarines....a lighthouse tour....walks in rural countryside....Department of National Defence exercise and mooring area....

Charts

3585 Nanoose Harbour and Approaches	1:16,700
3454 Gabriola Passage to Ballenas Island	1:40,000

Moorage In Nanoose Harbour, anchorage behind the breakwater[1] near the entrance to the harbour, or near the northwest shore;[2] Department of National Defence buoys and docks are out of bounds

At Schooner Cove,[3] limited anchorage or paid moorage at private floats

At Ballenas Island, a mooring buoy at the northern end; anchorage between the islands or in Boathouse Cove[4]

Facilities At Nanoose,[5] a hotel with licensed dining room and pub; post office

At Schooner Cove, a marina-and-condominium complex under construction

At Ballenas Islands, only the lighthouse station

At Northwest Bay,[6] complete marina services

Caution Winds in the open Strait can rise swiftly. Be wary of weather changes.

Keep clear of DND training manoeuvers.

Access Car access to Nanoose Harbour and to Schooner Cove

Launching ramps: Schooner Cove; Northwest Bay

Nanoose, a large and natural harbour without even a public float. A welcome change of pace. A place just to drop anchor and do simple things like rowing a dinghy through the river delta maze, picking berries along a quiet road, or climbing the north shore which rises in easy-going terraces to the peak of Nanoose Hill. Or just listening to the train whistle through the valley.

Beneath Nanoose Hill, a local swimming hole. The water of this cove is enticingly warm in summer, clear, and full of life. Sculpins in tidepools on a ledge. Oysters and clams. Purple shore crabs under every rock. Herring in underwater clouds. Flounders nervously skittering away, trailing dust tracks along the bottom.

A trail from the cove and up the bluff leads to a road which joins the Island Highway at Nanoose over two miles away. A good walk on pavement, past fields and forest and some spectacular flower gardens. And good reason to treat yourself to dinner or a beer at the hotel. You could, of course, anchor on that side of the harbour, and circumvent the walk.

Outside Nanoose Harbour, a downright desolate rash of rocks and reefs promises good fishing, and there's emergency shelter at Schooner Cove should the wind blow up.

North Ballenas is treasure island — riches for explorers. Moor between the islands, weather permitting. Animal trails lead from beach to underbrush; probably mink, by the spoor in the hollow. Strange to see cactus and oysters side by side along the shore. Follow the white dots painted on the rocks to find a giant cedar, an old well, and a trail between a boathouse ruin and Ballenas Lighthouse Station.

Miss the trail? Then scramble cross-country to discover split-rail fences, collapsed and weathered almost white, and a mysterious mound of round stones. Juniper trees and apple trees and a savanna of chest-high grass. And the remains of the old lighthouse at the island peak. A circle view here, and a breeze even on hot days.

Then there's Nanoose Island Light itself, and a guided tour if the keeper isn't busy: power plants and lifeboat-launching gear, radios and sophisticated weather-reporting devices. A fascinating look not only at a light station but at a unique way of life.

Did you know: The Canadian Coast Guard is responsible for marine safety along 16,000 miles of coastline in B.C.

Ballenas lighthouse

Roots and logs drift to Fegan Islets

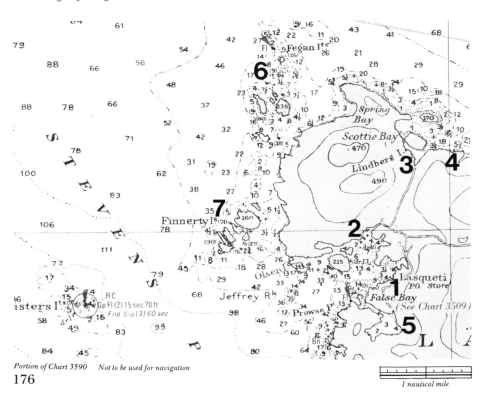

Portion of Chart 3590   Not to be used for navigation

1 nautical mile

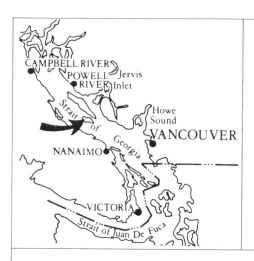

40

Northern Lasqueti Island

What's There rural way of life....clams....oysters....fish....prawns....wild edibles....fresh garden produce....deer and gone-wild sheep....wharf-side store and restaurant....ferry access, but not for cars....the Teapot House....

Charts

3509 large scale plans of False Bay	1:12,000
3590 Ballenas Island to Cape Lazo	1:77,000

Moorage At False Bay,[1] a public wharf open to a westerly swell; do not moor at the space reserved for the ferry

In Orchard Bay,[2] good anchorage

At Scottie Bay,[3] anchorage only, but very secure

Facilities At False Bay, fuel and water at the public wharf; phone, small general store with post office, and a some-time-open licensed restaurant

Taste the water before filling boat water tanks

Caution When crossing from the False Bay Wharf to the anchorage in Orchard Bay watch for the rock that dries at a 13-foot tide: each year it snags new samples of bottom paint.

Access By foot-passenger ferry from French Creek, on Vancouver Island, to False Bay

A visit to Lasqueti Island — next best to cruising the South Seas. Evergreens instead of palms, but easy living anyway. Cabins of "found" materials, with walkways of white oyster shells and driftwood fences to keep out the deer. People with a cheerful disregard for clothes on warm days. Great salmon fishing. Rockfish and cod, easy catches. Shellfish to be gathered with confidence: there's little to pollute them here. (The rare poisonous "red tides" excepting.) Enormous wild berries within yards of the wharf at False Bay, and more along the roadsides.

With a pocket guide to wild edibles, spend a day simply wandering. Nice walking on the gravel roads, because the island has few cars to kick up dust. Not far above False Bay, notice a distinctive house made of log rounds and capped with a teapot-shaped chimney. Admire the marvellous kitchen gardens, with their vegetables you didn't know existed. If unsuccessful at wild foraging, ask to buy strange squashes and exotic herbs.

Lasqueti has been mined and farmed and logged in overlapping layers. Look for old mining pits and burrows near the shorelines of False Bay, and in Barnes Cove[4] near Scottie Bay. But watch for sudden cave-ins caused by rotted timbers giving way. Domestic sheep have gone wild since the farmers have disappeared. And blacktail deer bound through the logged-off clearings.

Some natural features: a salt-water lagoon[3] opening into the south shore of False Bay has strange warm-water life forms; the outer guard of little islands, the Fegan[6] and Finnerty groups,[7] have wild flowers galore and gnarled driftwood, and collecting-pools of tidewater. And even cactus.

Always come to Lasqueti thinking that you might be trapped for days here by a sudden blow. Then Scottie Bay is the most secure place to be. A few houses and a private dock adding a touch of civilization, tame ducks begging handouts add company, and some of the best clam digging in the area, on nearby spits and beaches, bolstering your food supply. Being trapped here could be a pleasure.

Did you know: According to local legend, a gang of ruffians holed up on Lasqueti after a robbery at Union Bay, buried their loot and left it. Under a cedar tree. Somewhere on the island.

Marine Weather Reporting Stations in the Strait of Georgia

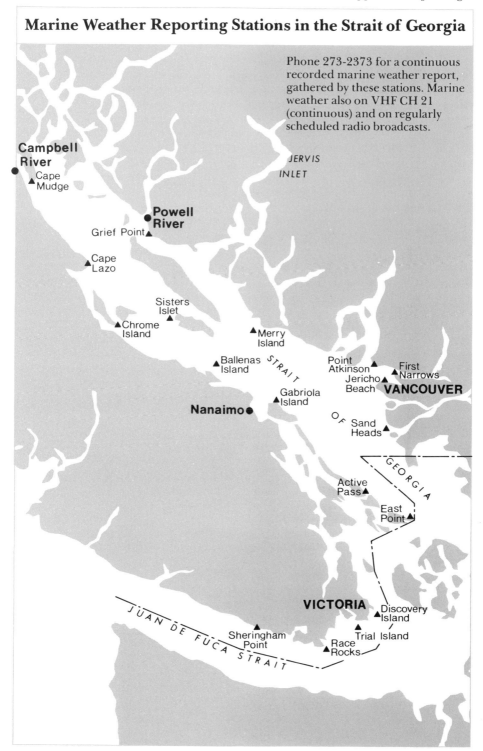

Phone 273-2373 for a continuous recorded marine weather report, gathered by these stations. Marine weather also on VHF CH 21 (continuous) and on regularly scheduled radio broadcasts.

JERVIS INLET

Campbell River
▲ Cape Mudge

Powell River
Grief Point ▲

▲ Cape Lazo

Sisters Islet ▲

▲ Chrome Island

▲ Merry Island

▲ Ballenas Island

STRAIT

Point Atkinson ▲
Jericho ▲ First Narrows ▲
Beach **VANCOUVER**

Gabriola ▲ Island

Nanaimo ●

OF

Sand ▲ Heads

GEORGIA

Active Pass ▲

East Point ▲

VICTORIA
Discovery ▲ Island

JUAN DE FUCA STRAIT

Sheringham ▲ Point

Trial Island

Race ▲ Rocks

179

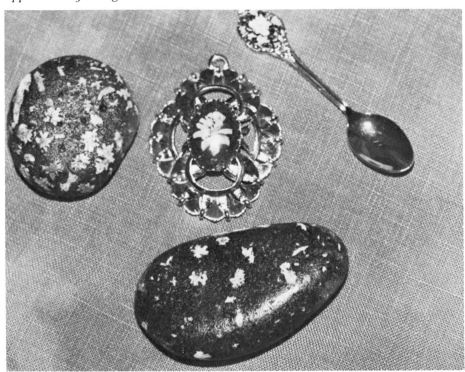

"Flower rock" from Gillies Bay

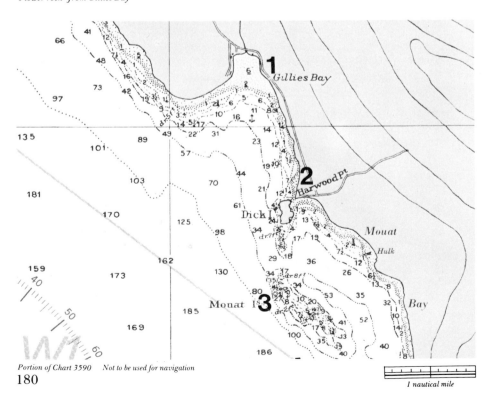

1 nautical mile

41

Gillies Bay

What's There beach-front community park....campsites....miles of pebble beach and driftwood....magnificent sunsets....wild berries....island deer....fishing...."flower rock"

Charts
3590 Ballenas Island to Cape Lazo   1:77,000

Moorage Only anchorage, and only temporary: exposed to any wind with west in it

Facilities At Gillies Bay community,[1] a general store, cafe, fresh baking, bank, gas station, medical clinic, resort with accommodation and small rental boats; liquor store several miles inland on the road to Blubber Bay

At Harwood Point Park,[2] campsites, tables, fire pits, drinking water, toilets, change room, phone and a summer concession stand; swings, grass, and horseshoe pitch

Caution For a slow boat, the run to better shelter is a long one, 12 miles southeast to Scottie Bay at Lasqueti Island.

Access By road via the Westview-to-Blubber Bay car ferry
     Launching ramp: Harwood Point Park

For small-boat camping and for trailer-boating, Gillies Bay is perfect. There's Harwood Point Park with its campsites and evergreens and grass and games and those marvellous miles and miles of beach. And there's the resort beside the park, for those who don't want to rough it.

At low tides walk along the beach from the park to the village for supplies and local gossip. At high tides enjoy the road instead: paved, so not dusty. Gillies Bay was a company town until the mine closed down in 1977. Still here are the houses, the machinery and tunnels a few miles north along the coast, and some of the people who live a simple and quiet way of life.

By water, Gillies Bay is remote, the only settlement along the entire west side of Texada; a shore grand and wild and mountainous from Mount Dick to Dick Island, but at Gillies Bay gentling to let you near. Mountains turn to hills, cliffs to coves, and waterfalls to creeks, but for all that gentleness, the bay lacks shelter. In a cruising boat, visit Gillies Bay in an afternoon, in calm and stable weather. If you can haul your boat ashore, don't worry that the bay is open to any western wind, or that the nearest good shelter is twelve miles away. Exciting, when your boat is safe ashore, to see waves breaking along the beach, and spray blowing across the Mouat Islets.[3] And open west-facing beaches have an undeniable advantage: a view to dazzling sunsets.

At Gillies Bay beachcombing means rockhounding. Especially for the striking "flower rock", the black porphyry with its bursts of white crystal blossoms. Even the most ordinary stones look special here: wave action grinds them to a jewel-stone perfection. Walking by the waterline when even a slight swell is running, you can hear the rhythmic rasp and scrape, a sound unique to pebble beaches: waves make a very efficient rock tumbler. Sleek black pebbles, icy white quartz, and rocks as pink and cool as popsicles. And a pocketful of "flower rock".

Did you know: Marble quarried on Texada was used to face the Vancouver Post Office.

Something to Try: Gathering Seaside Collectibles

Driftwood: Cut to the desired form, then smooth down the rough sections and sand the piece, using finer and finer grades of sandpaper. Finish with an application of wood oil, varnish, shellac or wax. Or stain the wood with shoe polish. Prefer the natural approach? Shape and smooth the surface of the driftwood with the tip of a deer horn — another collectible to find — and use dogfish skin for any necessary sanding; then oil the wood by rubbing it against your skin.

Fossils: Look for fossils in sandstone cliffs and in shaly banks along the shorelines formed in layers of sand or mud or gravel, and where creatures and plants of long ago might have been buried and preserved. Look around Hornby and Sucia Islands, for instance. Use an old toothbrush to remove grit gently from the fossil surface.

Rocks: With a field guide to rockhounding, expect to make interesting discoveries of minerals, crystals and gemstones almost anywhere along the coast. Certain areas feature special "finds": look for "flower rock" at Gillies Bay, pink granite at Cortes Bay, pink rhodonite at Fulford Harbour, dallasite on Victoria beaches not far from Dallas Road, after which the rock was named.

Sand: Gather a sampling of sand from every sandy beach you visit. Displayed in small glass vials, such as those in which you buy cake decorations, these samplings will amaze you with their difference in colours and textures. Even something as simple as sand can be a variable collectible!

Sounds: Collect a collage of seaside sounds with a tape recorder. Seagulls mewling. The crunch of footsteps on a gravel beach. Wind whistling through the rigging. Waves breaking. The splashing of swimmers. The excitement of a fish being landed. The snap of sails.

Don't be thoughtless with your gathering. Disturb seaside creatures as little as possible in your search for collectibles. And if you find anything obviously unique or special — archaeological remains and artifacts — take a picture, and leave the find where it is. The nearest museum will be glad to hear about it.

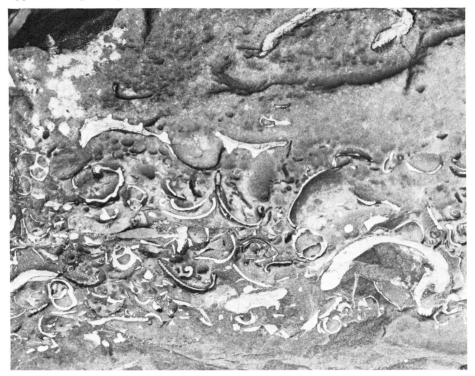

Fossils near Ford Cove

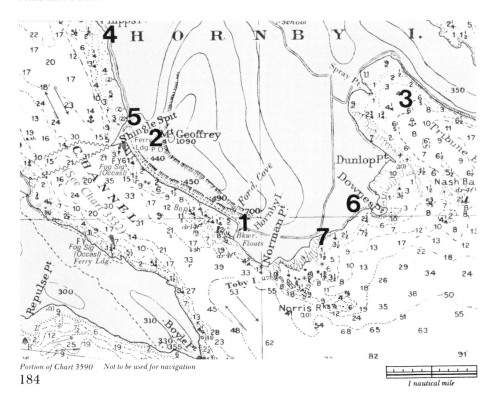

Portion of Chart 3590   Not to be used for navigation

1 nautical mile

42

Southern Hornby Island

What's There fossils....rockhounding....shellfish....Indian rock carvings....neighbourhood pub....good small-boat camping....cliff side trail....berry picking....locally-made pottery....

Charts

3532 Baynes Sound and Approaches	1:40,000
3590 Ballenas Island to Cape Lazo	1:77,000

Moorage At Ford Cove,[1] a public wharf and good anchorage behind a breakwater

At Shingle Spit[2] and at Tribune Bay,[3] temporary anchorage only

Facilities At Ford Cove, fuel and water at the wharf, some groceries at the store; campsite nearby

At Shingle Spit, resort facilities including laundry and showers, cabins, campsites, groceries and neighbourhood pub

At Tribune Bay, a resort, campsites, co-op store, horseback riding

Caution A long drying reef parallels the shore at the entrance to Ford Cove. Approach the wharf through the gap between the end of the breakwater and the black spar buoy.

Access By car from Vancouver Island via ferry from Buckley Bay to Denman Island, and another ferry from Denman to Shingle Spit on Hornby Island

Launching ramp: Shingle Spit

To enjoy rockhounding on Hornby Island, you don't have to know much about rocks. Only that their colours are often beautiful, their shapes interesting, and their variety astounding. Look for agates, garnets, jasper and dallasite along the beaches. Or a concretion: a formation of one rock within another, so that you don't know what you have until you break it open. A sort of rock surprise.

There are the layers of an ancient beach, with pebbles, sand, shells and sand again, all moulded into one boulder. An oyster shell shows one edge free. Feel the smooth inside of it, and the rough outside complete with barnacles. All fossilized.

Spend time exploring the shorelines near Ford Cove, especially at low tide. At some places the sandstone is as smooth as pavement; at others it's pitted and honeycombed, holding tidepools in hollows big enough to bathe in. And some parts of the shore are heaped with strange conglomerate rock shapes, as though loads of cement were poured over a pebble beach, stirred up, and left to dry into pillars, piles and slabs.

Do things ancient and historical intrigue you? Indian graves and stone tools were found at Shingle Spit. The remains of Indian fish traps at Phipps Point.[4] A pioneer cemetery at Graveyard Point.[5] Petroglyphs — Indian rock carvings — at Downes Point[6] and, one more difficult to find, on Ford Creek.[7]

Tribune Bay has a beautiful beach, but best not to anchor overnight in the bay: many a boat has dragged its anchor ashore when an unexpected south wind blew up. After all, if it weren't for wind and rough water, the beach and the sandstone caves would not have been carved out.

Follow the road from Tribune Bay to Ford Cove for some magnificent vistas out over the strait, with storybook farms in the foreground. On one side of the road, forest and moss and craggy hillside; on the other, fences and lush fields, and hummocks and hollows unbelievably green.

And a really pleasant walking trail starts by the beach at Ford Cove and follows the cliffs about a mile to Shingle Spit. Blackberry bushes fence in part of the road near Ford Cove Store, and the berries grow along the upper reaches of the beach. A unique taste treat: sun-warmed berries washed in salt water. Parts of the trail are wide and grassy; other parts are single-file narrow, mere footholds in the cliffside. The old roadway has slipped down to the beach below, in places a disconcertingly long way. But most of the trail is easy walking, and always within sight of Lambert Channel. There's a resort at Shingle Spit, with restaurant and a neighbourhood pub. A cool beer after a scenic walk: good planning!

Did you know: The teredo, or shipworm, is really a wood-boring clam.

Wild, Wild Berry Recipes

Rose Blossom Tea: Add a handful of rose blossoms to a billycan of water and boil 10 minutes. Let steep, and sweeten to taste.

Rose Hip Tea: Pour a palmful of rose hips, with their blossom ends picked off, into a billycan of boiling water, and let steep about 10 minutes. Sweeten to taste.

Rose Hip Jelly: Boil rose hips in a small amount of water until the hips are tender. Mash them, and press the pulp through a sieve or clean cloth. Measure the strained pulp, and add an equal amount of sugar. Boil mixture hard, until a sampling taken on a spoon will jell. Allow to cool. Especially good served with fish.

Berry Drink: Those berries containing too many pips, or those not tasty enough or not plentiful enough to eat out of hand, make into a refreshing drink. Mash the berries into their own juice, and stir in about a cupful of water for every cupful of berry mash. Let stand overnight. Strain through a clean, thin cloth, and dilute with more water if desired. Add sugar to taste. Try a mix of several kinds of berries.

Berry Topping: Mash berries into their own juice. You may have to add a bit of water to start the juice flowing. If the berries contain too many pips, strain the mash through a clean, thin cloth. To every cupful of pulpy juice, add 1 tablespoon of cornstarch (or 2 of flour) combined with 2 tablespoons of sugar. Bring the mixture to a boil, and stir constantly until it is clear and thick. Serve over pancakes or pudding.

Berry Pancakes: Try adding sweet wild berries to pancake batter.

Hint: When gathering berries that you don't wish squished, place them in a plastic bag, blow into the bag, and seal it securely. The berries will be air-cushioned against damage.

salmonberry

wild rose

Conning up quiet Courtenay River

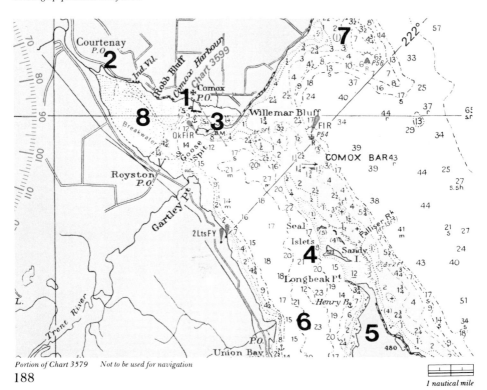

Portion of Chart 3579   Not to be used for navigation

1 nautical mile

43

Courtenay and Comox

What's There two cities within three miles....a river cruise....fresh-water moorage....extensive small-boat harbour....islets of sand and mud to explore....good fishing near Cape Lazo....Canadian Armed Forces Base....Sea Cadets....

Charts

3599 Comox Harbour	1:10,000
3532 Baynes Sound and Approaches	1:40,000

Moorage At Comox Harbour,[1] extensive float footage at the public wharf behind a breakwater, and good anchorage nearby

At Courtenay Slough,[2] during the summer when fishboats are not moored there, public floats in fresh water

Entrance to the slough is across a 2.4 metre high (8 feet) concrete sill

Facilities At Comox, cruising and repair facilities including a tide grid (see wharfinger)

At Courtenay, most general supplies including a well-stocked hardware store

Caution Going toward the slough, navigate the Courtenay River[8] with care and on a rising tide. Pay attention to the range markers and watch for snags alongside the channel.

Access By boat or car

Launching ramps: Comox; Courtenay

To consider Comox as merely a convenient supply stop is to overlook a really delightful cruising area. Which isn't to say that Comox isn't a good place to re-stock. It is. The harbour large and protected, moorage at the public wharf arranged in a businesslike way, and general facilities, from laundromat to liquor store, nearby.

Comox sports a jaunty military air. In the summer, Sea Cadets train at the base on Goose Spit,[9] just a trumpet blast from town and wharf. You'll sleep and wake to the notes of taps and reveille, and at the wharf when the wind is right you'll plainly hear officers of vigourous voice. The Cadets' maneuvers in their fleet of open boats, an entertaining show. A Cadet parade — complete with cannon and a rousing marching band — a Comox summer feature.

Comox boasts of sandy beaches, enticing on a hot day, but in any weather the undeveloped provincial park of Sandy Island and Seal Islet[4] is perfect for picnics. These islands shrink and swell amazingly, depending on the tide. Sometimes they are mere spots on the bar between Denman Island[5] and Comox, the permanently dry parts knitted together with scrub brush, wild flowers, and bits of rusty barbed wire left from war-time training exercises. At lower tide, walk, or at least wade, from mound to sandy mound, an intertidal exhibition at your feet: strange swimming, skittering "things" caught in little tidepools, and swamp gardens of seaweed.

From the south and under sail in Baynes Sound,[6] the approach to Comox can be a fantastic run of fifteen miles along green and gentle shores. Approaching from the north, be glad to cross Comox Bar and leave the Strait of Georgia behind, especially when a southeaster shoves the Strait around. Good fishing near Cape Lazo,[7] but when a wind blows up even commercial fishermen are glad to cross back to the comparative calm of Baynes Sound.

The Courtenay River,[8] navigable to most boats on a high, rising tide, leads to one of the most hidden, peaceful, public moorings along the coast. Just go slowly, keeping your eyes on the markers and ranges.

The passage is alluring. Past mud flats close enough to touch. Great blue herons stalking along the shallows. A family of harbour seals. Past the hulks and drying nets and fishing gear on the Indian Reserve. Past the highway, an airstrip and a sawmill. Then the river becomes a canal along lawns and little jetties and overhanging trees. Look down to see clearly every pebble on the river bottom.

Look for the entrance to the slough moorage basin through a tree-shaded gap on your starboard side, a stone's throw before the bridge. The basin is a storage place for fishboats in winter, but in summer the floats are almost empty. At night the scents of fresh-cut grass and not-so-distant farms overcome the tang of salt air: you have unmistakably voyaged inland.

Did you know: "The Lorne", oldest licensed pub-hotel in the province, near Comox public wharf, displays some interesting old photographs of the area.

Some Handy Knots

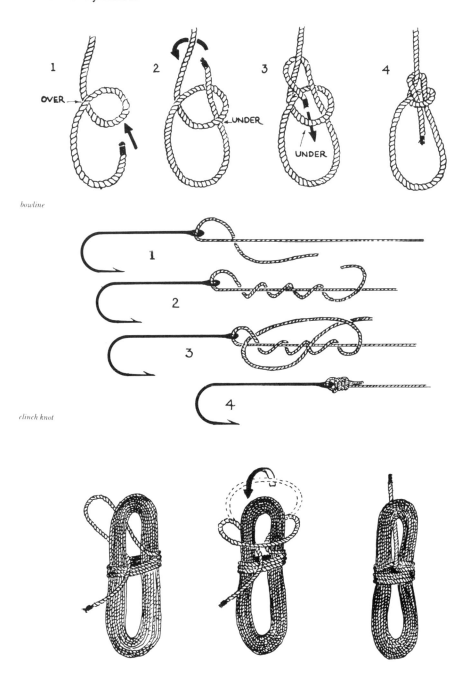

bowline

clinch knot

coiling line

Chapter Six
Desolation Sound and Discovery Islands

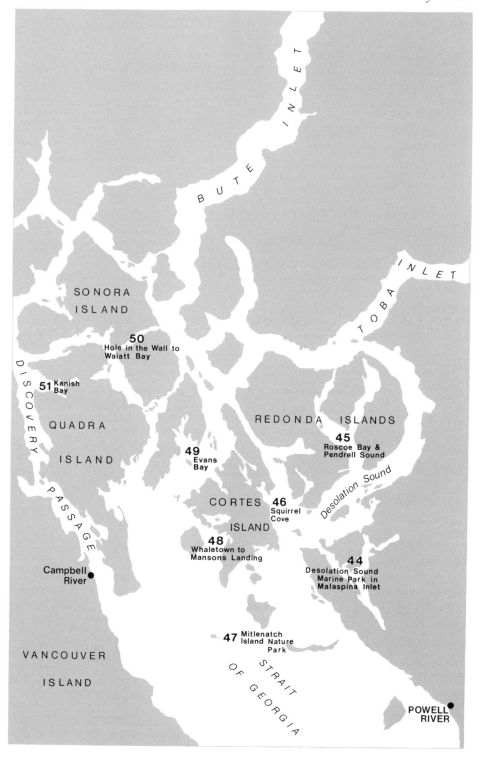

BUTE INLET

TOBA INLET

SONORA
ISLAND

50
Hole in the Wall to
Waiatt Bay

51 Kanish
Bay

DISCOVERY

QUADRA

ISLAND

PASSAGE

Campbell
River

REDONDA ISLANDS

45
Roscoe Bay &
Pendrell Sound

49
Evans
Bay

Desolation Sound

CORTES **46**
Squirrel
Cove

ISLAND

48
Whaletown to
Mansons Landing

44
Desolation Sound
Marine Park in
Malaspina Inlet

VANCOUVER

ISLAND

47 Mitlenatch
Island Nature
Park

STRAIT
OF
GEORGIA

POWELL
RIVER

Old logging machinery at Grace Harbour

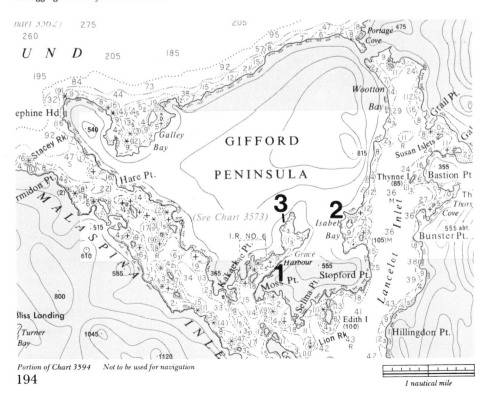

1 nautical mile

44

Desolation Sound Marine Park in Malaspina Inlet

What's There south border of the largest marine park in B.C.....extremely sheltered water......swimming, hiking, canoeing, exploring....undeveloped shorelines....clams....oysters....beaver dams and little lakes....

Charts

3573 Malaspina Inlet	1:12,600
3562 Redonda Islands	1:37,600

Moorage In Grace Harbour[1] and in Isabel Bay,[2] excellent anchorage

Many other spots good for temporary anchorage

Facilities None, in this undeveloped part of the inlet

At Okeover Inlet about 3 miles south, phone, restaurant, store and campsite near the public wharf

Caution Because of drying rocks and several reefs, navigate Malaspina Inlet with close attention to chart and to tide tables. Tidal currents may reach 2 knots at the entrance of the inlet.

Access By boat only

Nearest car access to the public wharf, at Okeover Inlet

Nearest launching ramp: Okeover Inlet

Here, gunkholing at its finest: inlets within inlets, bays and coves and islets within those. Chances are you'll find an anchorage to yourself. Even in the busy cruising season many boaters miss this offshoot of Desolation Sound. All the more pleasant for those who do find it: quiet water guaranteed. Strong winds blowing in the Strait are of no concern here. Malaspina Peninsula blocks the worst of winds, and the turns and twists of the inlets — and the many little islands — deflect the land breezes. Lee shores all the way!

The water warms invitingly in summer. Just right for swimming; and the snorkelling is irresistible. Oysters are the proof of warm water: they won't breed where it's cold. Several oyster farms work foreshore leases along the inlet, but there's free picking where the shores aren't posted.

Most of all, this cruise is for exploring. Walk a short way inland from Grace Harbour to a small lake[3] ringed with lily pads and sunken logs, and shaped by beaver dams. The lake shore too marshy for swimming, but sit on a knoll covered in deep moss and watch some of the day go by. Bring a picnic lunch, and stay to listen to the loons.

Poke through old settlements for fascinating piles of junk. At Isabel Bay some collapsed cabins and traces of garden walls and pathways mark a settlement. An apple tree shaded by firs, and garden flowers mixed with sword fern. Was this deserted five, or fifty years ago? Hard to say, but fun to look for clues.

Find old landings, old roads, old tokens of logging. By Grace Harbour, a tree grows through the skeleton of a caterpillar tractor, and bits of the machine spread, like puzzle pieces, throughout the underbrush. Links of tread, pistons, cogs, and bits of chain, all rust-fused and dull as dirt. Any metallic shininess is on the salal leaves hiding the segments.

Piece it all together: not just the machines, but the noise and action in a Malaspina Inlet shoreline logging camp. There a line of grown alder marks a skid road. On this tree a lumpy scar shows where a cable choked the bark. Follow the chain-bruises to the waterline where a root pins down part of a hobnail boot. An antique beer bottle buried to the neck beside a trail.

Did you know: Malaspina Inlet was named after "Capitan de Navio" Alexandro Malaspina, born 1754, an Italian in the Spanish navy.

Something to Try: Hunting Old Bottles

Squat bottles, square bottles; bottles fragile, bulbous, lumpy or long, in curious shapes and gemstone colours. Amethyst. Opaline. Emerald. Cobalt blue. Ink bottles, canning jars, opium bottles, whiskey jugs. Oddly shaped bottles often held medicines because they could be easily identified, even in the dark. Look for bottles with coarse thick glass, with bubbles, and with crooked seams. Imperfections add value. Bottles without seams were hand blown: often oldest, and most rare.

Old bottles can be treasures to collectors, but are fun for anyone to find. The coastline is a bottle hunter's dream, with the deserted settlements so easy to find from seaward. A bit of detective work then to uncover the building sites and garbage pits. Look for bottles in gullies, under rock piles, in crawlspaces, behind outbuildings, near boat landings. Liquor bottles were often stashed by an outhouse: convenient spot for a secret nip.

Don't overlook bottle sites which might seem just too obvious: one collector unearthed an attractive Chinese pot from an empty lot beside the fuel dock at Egmont, a place many would think too public, too "gone over". On the other hand, bottles turn up in the unlikeliest of spots: a fine old beer bottle in a beaver dam. A logger had left it there, maybe. Or had the beaver?

Old bottles tend to be brittle and break easily. Hot water can shatter them as surely as can a hammer blow. Clean an old bottle carefully:

Use a stick to rub off the surface dirt. A knife might scratch the glass.

Pour some water and a handful of sand into the bottle, and shake to scour the inside.

Soak the bottle in a solution of sudsy ammonia. For days if necessary. During the soaking period, occasionally work at the grime with a bottle brush.

Clean stubbornly dirty or barnacled bottles by soaking them in a 2% solution of muriatic acid and water, and then use tin oxide to polish the glass. Many collectors, though, would rather the glass be rough, with barnacles and all. A matter of taste.

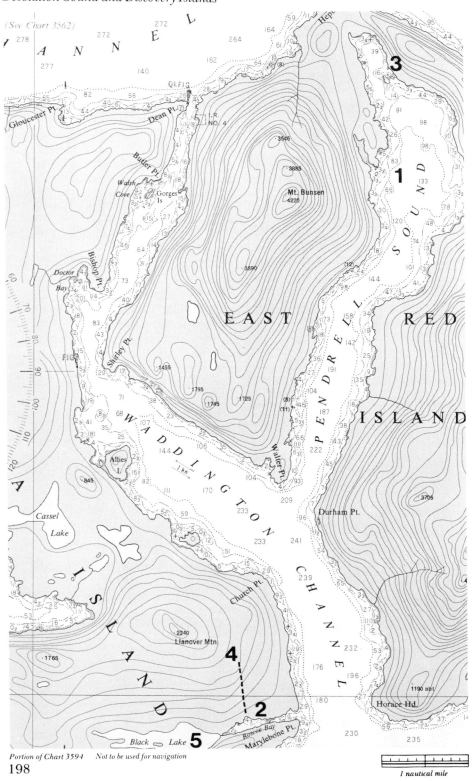

1 nautical mile

45

Roscoe Bay and Pendrell Sound

What's There warmest water in Desolation Sound....a very sheltered little bay....fresh-water swimming....trout fishing....hike to a panoramic view....a look at different methods of oyster spat collection....a lake within dinghy-carrying distance....

Charts

3562 Redonda Islands	1:37,500
3594 Discovery Passage, Toba Inlet and connecting channels	1:75,000

Moorage In Pendrell Sound,[1] anchorage limited because few spots offer both protection from winds and water shallow enough

In Roscoe Bay,[2] good anchorage; the floats are private, belonging to a logging company which stores boomsticks in the bay; some boats tie to the booms

Facilities None: nearest supplies and radiotelephone at Refuge Cove, on the southwest side of West Redonda Island

Also at Refuge Cove: showers, laundry, fuel, liquor, charts, and a good supply of books and publications

Caution The bar in the middle of the entrance to Roscoe Bay is awash at low water: cross on a rising tide.

Note: Speed limit in Pendrell Sound is 4 knots to minimize boat wash that could interfere with the oyster culture structures.

Access By boat only

Nearest launching ramps: Lund; Okeover Inlet

Water temperatures up to 25.6 C (78°F) — on the surface at least — make Pendrell Sound the warmest spot in Desolation Sound. Irresistible for swimming. Pendrell, with its uniquely warm and unpolluted water, is an ideal ecological reserve for oyster culture, the most important oyster spat nursery in the province. The oyster spat, or seed, collected here re-stocks commercial oyster beds. A captivating variety of methods for the collection of the spat: empty oyster shells, gathered in nets or threaded in clusters and hung from rafts; specially designed "collars" and "caps" suspended from miles of line held up by hundreds of floats; and tiers of trays piled up in shallow water. Boaters are welcome to come for a close look, so long as they don't disturb the delicate spat-collecting structures. Obey the 4-knot speed limit.

Strangely, few large plump oysters are found in Pendrell Sound. The conditions so perfect for oyster breeding discourage oyster growth. The competition for feed is too great here, and the baby oysters must be shipped to other beaches for final fattening.

Look for the rusty-red designs of Indian rock paintings on a cliff near the end of the Sound.[3]

Pendrell Sound, for a lazy afternoon exploring, but Roscoe Bay for a made-to-order anchorage. A word of caution: the entrance to the bay snags several boats a week during cruising season; you must enter on a flooding tide to prevent being left high and dry in full view of everyone in the anchorage. In the bay, a waterfall courses down a rock face, the water sliding down long green streamers of algae and splashing onto an oyster-covered ledge. Oysters, like cruising boats in summer, anchored in clumps, fastened to each other.

A rough road[4] behind the logging camp leads up and up and up to a glorious view — deep into Pendrell Sound and far over the islands of Prideaux Haven. About an hour each way, with stops for rest and berry picking.

Walk from Roscoe Bay to Black Lake,[5] along an outflow so short that you can easily carry your dinghy along the path. And don't forget to bring a trout rod. The shoreline of the lake is a logged-over tangle. Row to the far end of the lake, to a spooky "Everglades" of half-drowned trees and hanging moss and swampy weeds. Crocodiles would be at home here! Or stop on the island at the centre of the lake, on an idyllic bit of rock and grass and wild flowers surrounded by shallow shelves of water blissfully soft and warm in summer.

Did you know:
Oysters can live for twenty years and can weigh more than a kilogram — up to two and a half pounds.

About Oysters

Oysters are intertidal creatures and not the least bit shy about it: they don't burrow, crawl, or swim away. They just lie there, proof that some of the best things in life can be easy picking.

Most oysters found in the foreshores of the Strait of Georgia and Puget Sound are the imported Japanese variety which, after being introduced to these waters, quickly replaced the smaller, slower-growing native Olympia oyster. An oyster can spawn as a male one year, a female the next, producing millions of eggs in one season. Only a fraction of the eggs become fertilized and fewer yet survive their first weeks of floating free with the currents. The spat, or young oysters, that do survive eventually wash to shore where they fasten themselves to a smooth surface. There they stay for life, sometimes growing to a foot long.

For eating, most people prefer smaller, younger oysters, whose innards don't look quite so specifically like innards. When to eat an oyster? Anytime, in months with or without an "R". True, oysters in the cold-water months are more plump and solid than during the summer spawning time, and the bloom of summer plankton gives oysters a greenish tinge and a slightly iodine taste, but these are harmless effects. Enjoy oysters safely:

Be aware of "red tide" notices and "shellfish pollution" signs. Don't take oysters from beaches near sources of raw sewage.

Keep oysters alive until you cook them. They will live for days if kept cool and moist in a shady place under a wet sack.

Leave shucked oyster shells on the beach: they provide a base for next years' spat.

Take no more than your legal limit. And don't pick oysters on commercial oyster leases.

Rafts of cultch for oyster spat

Derelict at Squirrel Cove

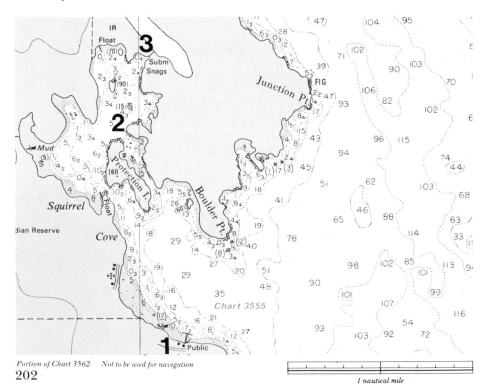

1 nautical mile

46
Squirrel Cove

What's There undeveloped marine park....beached boat hulk....small settlement....warm water for swimming....salt-water lagoon....exciting dinghy rides on a tidal creek....

Charts

3555 large scale plans of Squirrel Cove	1:12,000
3562 Redonda Islands	1:37,500
3563 Sutil Channel to Stuart Island	1:37,500

Moorage At Squirrel Cove settlement,[1] a public wharf with floats, but lack of protection from winds and waves makes this an uneasy overnight tie-up

   Within Squirrel Cove[2] itself, excellent anchorage

Facilities At Squirrel Cove settlement, post office, phone and general store with liquor

   No fuel available at Squirrel Cove; nearest fuel at Cortes Bay to the south or at Refuge Cove across the channel

Caution To avoid being grounded in Squirrel Cove, take careful depth soundings before anchoring and make allowance for the extra distance your boat will swing at lower tides.

Access By car to Squirrel Cove settlement via car ferry from Campbell River and Quadra Island to Whaletown, Cortes Island

   Nearest launching ramp: Mansons Landing

A miniature white-water course[3] for dinghies is the attraction in Squirrel Cove. A tidal creek. The cove and the lagoon pour back and forth with the changing tides and the ride on the stream is a thrill, especially when the creek is all rocks and rapids. For adventurers only. You can, of course, go through when the lagoon is full and the stream is decorously deep and slow; then you have time to explore and to slip out with the reversed stream.

The lagoon is a world apart. Water very still and warm in summer. So much strange life in the shallows that you seem to be rowing on the surface of an aquarium. Islets seem there purely for decoration, to display trees as stunted and twisted as Japanese bonsai.

Without a chart, you can easily miss the entrance to Squirrel Cove: the passage is almost invisible until you're in it. Then, even with a chart to warn you, the size of the cove surprises: a suddenly-opening space of perfect protection. The shores form little bays, with island dividers. Space enough for a dozen boats to anchor, each hidden from the other. And space enough for a hundred boats to find shelter, rafted four and five together. A surprise, then, to see a sleek and sumptuous river otter hunting along the quiet shore.

Outside, Squirrel Cove Indian Reserve is a photogenic scattering of pastel-painted houses and a steepled church. The post office, general store and wharf knit up Squirrel Cove settlement. The post office near the wharf a patchwork shed so small and gray and weathered that it can only be called colourful. The store with an interesting selection of stock: mundane household goods for residents and some luxurious frills for cruising customers. Several times each week, a flurry of activity at the wharf: the mail plane lands.

At low tide explore the old boat hulk beached near the settlement. Weathering and wave action are more slowly but more surely breaking down the parts of the ship that resisted stripping, burning and even dynamiting.

Did you know: A sea cucumber can disgorge its insides, and stay alive to grow a new set of internal organs.

Provincial Marine Parks in Discovery Islands and Desolation Sound

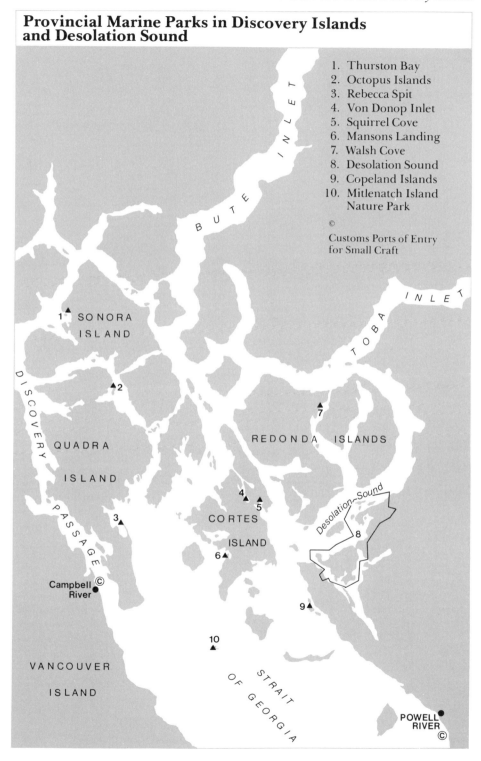

1. Thurston Bay
2. Octopus Islands
3. Rebecca Spit
4. Von Donop Inlet
5. Squirrel Cove
6. Mansons Landing
7. Walsh Cove
8. Desolation Sound
9. Copeland Islands
10. Mitlenatch Island
    Nature Park

© Customs Ports of Entry for Small Craft

BUTE INLET

TOBA INLET

1 SONORA ISLAND

2

7

REDONDA ISLANDS

DISCOVERY PASSAGE

QUADRA ISLAND

4
5

Desolation-Sound

8

CORTES ISLAND

3

6

Campbell © River

9

10

VANCOUVER ISLAND

STRAIT OF GEORGIA

POWELL RIVER ©

Bird blind at Mitlenatch Island

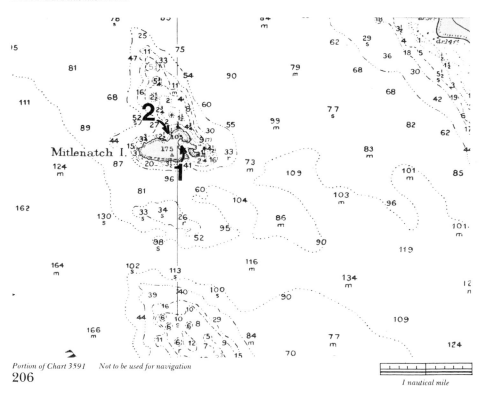

1 nautical mile

47

Mitlenatch Island Nature Park

What's There nature park and bird sanctuary....cactus and meadow flowers....self-guiding trails....park naturalist....pebble beach and picnic site....bird blind....

Charts
3591 Cape Lazo to Discovery Passage   1:76,400

Moorage Temporary anchorage only

Facilities Picnic table, pit toilet, trails, bird blind, naturalist tours during the cruise season; no drinking water

Caution Because the island offers no supplies and limited protection, this is not the place to go during uncertain weather. For small, slow boats the run to shelter is a long one.

Note: Do not interfere with any of the plant or animal life on Mitlenatch Island. Marine life is protected within the park boundaries, which extend 304.8 metres (1000 feet) from shore.

Access By boat only

Mitlenatch Island: so special that in 1961 it became a provincial nature park with park naturalists to study the unique life on the island and to explain its natural history to visitors.

What's there? Believe it or not, a desert island. A strange and wonderful place with cactus growing near the tide line, bluffs fringed with Garry oak, and with pine which did not grow here until 1958, when the latest of a series of fires changed the chemical composition of the soil just enough to foster such growth. A dry island, yet a natural garden. A valley full of meadow flowers: fireweed, tiger lilies, harebells, hyacinth and honeysuckle. Even a rare spired orchid. A natural pasture, not surprisingly once used for summering sheep and cattle: one farmer ferried his sheep here, rowing them two by two from Cortes.

And animal life. Thousands of deermice. Garter snakes that grow to three feet long. Otter burglarizing the nests of birds. Seals, whales and sea lions in nearby waters. Oysters in the little bay. And for divers, abalone — to see but not to take.

And birds! Truly a birdwatcher's paradise: a park checklist names 121 species — from hummingbirds to turkey vultures. Free-wheeling gulls fill the sky with their screaking, and a bird blind near the north bluffs allows a close look at the interior politics of a gull colony. Straggly lines of cormorants stand along the cliffs. Hawks and eagles drift lazily on the up-drafts over Mitlenatch.

Land at the little bay by the naturalist's cabin[1] where oysters lie thick along the shore. Or land at the northwest beach[2] where pebbles are smoothly ground and colourful, and where tide wrack tangles around a picnic table. A trail crosses the island between these two points, and branches off toward the bird blind. Take a camera, binoculars, and picnic lunch ashore.

Did you know: Near Mitlenatch is a point where flooding tides from the north meet the flooding tides from the south.

Birds that Nest on Mitlenatch Island....

pigeon guillemot

pelagic cormorant

black oystercatcher

Drawings by Mark Wynja

Sand and pine at Hague Lake

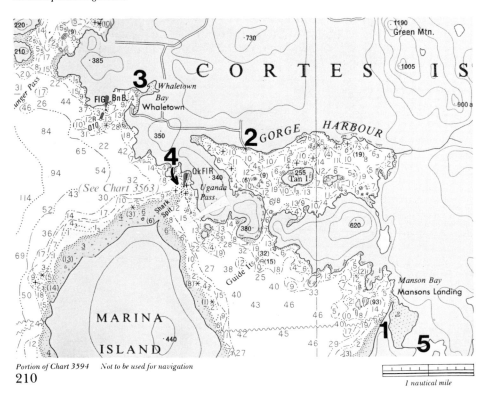

1 nautical mile

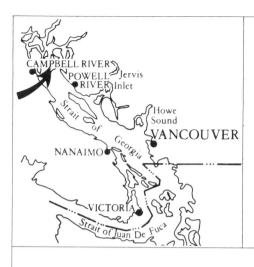

48

Whaletown to Mansons Landing

What's There pictographs and petroglyphs....island walks....fishing....beachcombing....small-boat camping....small island settlements....beach-front provincial park....resort restaurant....white sand beach on fresh-water lake....

Charts

3563 Sutil Channel to Stuart Island	1:37,500
3594 Discovery Passage, Toba Inlet and connecting channels	1:75,000

Moorage At Mansons Landing,[1] a public wharf with floats and nearby temporary anchorage

At Gorge Harbour,[2] moorage at the resort, and limited space at a small float at the public wharf; very protected anchorage, but on rocky bottom

At Whaletown,[3] a public wharf with floats; limited anchorage nearby

Facilities At Mansons Landing, a fuel dock, water, groceries and post office

Mansons Landing Marine Park: 117 acres, undeveloped

At Gorge Harbour, a resort-marina with restaurant, campground, showers, coin laundry, some boating supplies

At Whaletown, fuel, water, groceries, phone and post office

Caution When approaching Uganda Pass[4] from the east keep the red conical buoys on your starboard (right) side and turn around the black marker, keeping it on your port (left) side to avoid Shark Spit.

Access By car via ferry from Campbell River to Quadra Island to Whaletown Bay

Launching ramp: Mansons Landing

A few minutes walk from Mansons Landing, Hague Lake is a perfect travel-poster lake complete with white sand beaches and a border of pine forest. Follow the paved road from the store to the first intersection, then turn left. A provincial park sign points out the trail leading to the lake. Clear, fresh water. A welcome change from ocean swimming.

The entrance to Gorge Harbour is a spectacular narrow gash between cliffs. Look up to the cliff on the left to see Indian pictographs, some just shapes and symbols, but one seems to be of a man riding a whale. Once you recognize the rust-red markings you'll spot them easily at many places along the coast, usually in settings as dramatic as this. Seals often hunt in the Gorge, struggling with salmon of enviable size. Less lucky, you might have to resort to cod, which come willingly enough.

Uganda Pass, a puzzle of port hand and starboard hand markers, picks a way around Shark Spit. The spit almost disappears from view at high water, but at low tides is safe for beach fires. The people living on these islands are understandably worried about forest fires. Please be cautious.

Whaletown is a good, scenic, supply stop for boaters: the floats aren't usually too crowded; you'll find a general store, post office, church and a tiny library; and overlooking the wharf, the brightest flower garden on the island.

You can't really miss when cruising near any part of Cortes Island, but here especially the island offers an incredible variety. Three different bays with moorage. Two stores and a marine resort. Good fishing for bottom fish or salmon. Oysters, clams, crabs. Swimming in salt water or fresh. Exploring rocky islands, sandy spits, or country roads. A salt-water lagoon at Mansons Landing for a dinghy or canoe. A restaurant at Gorge Harbour. Indian pictographs in the Gorge, and a petroglyph on the beach south of Mansons Landing. Where else such variety in a five-mile stretch of coastline?

Did you know: Whaletown was a busy whaling station in 1869, but by 1872 the humpback whale had been hunted to scarcity in the Strait of Georgia.

Galley Chemistry

— Warmed vinegar will remove varnish from glass.

— Use a solution of vinegar and water to wipe salt rime off foul-weather gear. Also good for sparkling-up varnished surfaces, and glass covered with salty rime.

— Someone seasick? Use a vinegar-and-water solution to clean up after. The vinegar helps prevent stains on carpets and cushions, and removes unpleasant odours. Rinse well with fresh clean water.

— A splash of vinegar on a wet wiping cloth cuts the greasy film which tends to collect on galley surfaces. Use it on paint, varnish, glass, counters....

— Try a few drops of lemon juice instead of vinegar for wiping galley surfaces: leaves a delightfully fresh scent and cuts grease as well.

— Save squeezed-out lemon halves in a plastic bag: rub a piece of lemon over your hands after handling fish to remove odour from your skin.

— A solution of baking soda and water used to wipe out ice box, fridge, or "head" will prevent a build-up of odours.

— Keep a container of baking soda by the galley stove to douse small flare-ups, especially those involving grease. But also keep a fire extinguisher handy.

— Add a few dozen grains of uncooked rice to salt containers to absorb dampness and keep the salt free-flowing.

— To clean badly burned pots and dishes with baked-on food, spread an ammonia-soaked paper towel over the dirty surface, and place the entire pan or dish inside a plastic bag. Seal securely. Leave overnight, preferably outside in case ammonia fumes leak out. The dish should then rinse clean.

— Add a sprinkling of salt when cooking bitter berries to decrease the amount of sugar needed to make the fruit palatable.

— When cooking rice or noodles, add a tablespoon of cooking oil to the water to prevent it from readily foaming up and boiling over.

Country lane from Evans Bay to Surge Narrows

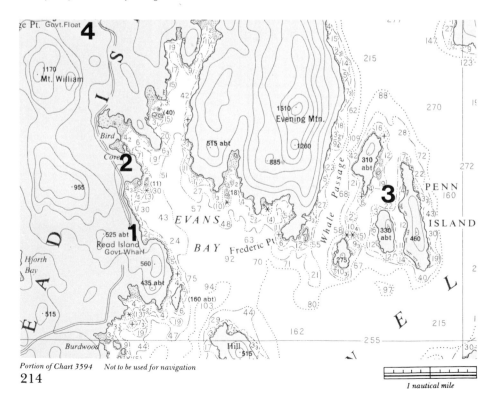

1 nautical mile

49

Evans Bay

What's There country road under giant cedars....eagles and sand dollars....clams....crabs....cod and rockfish and red snapper....whales in Whale Passage....

Charts

3563 Sutil Channel to Stuart Island	1:37,500
3594 Discovery Passage, Toba Inlet and connecting channels	1:75,000

Moorage At Evans Bay,[1] a public wharf with floats; anchorage in Bird Cove[2]

Facilities At Read Island settlement near the public wharf, a store with small stocks of groceries and fuel; fresh water

More complete facilities at Heriot Bay on Quadra Island, or at Whaletown on Cortes Island, each about 8 miles away

Caution Watch for drying rocks close to the shore in Evans Bay.

Access By boat only

Nearest launching ramp: Heriot Bay

Read Island is a place of eagles. They wheel slowly on the air currents above the shorelines; they perch on stark branches leaning over Evans Bay; an eyrie crowns a tall dead tree at the south end of the Penn Islands.[3] Look for bare, gray trees: you'll see eagles on the topmost branches. Something as large as an eagle doesn't look for camouflage.

The many eagles create a feeling of being far, far north of civilization. But perhaps the feeling comes from the sightings of whales and porpoises. If nothing else, the water itself has a northern coldness: it certainly doesn't invite swimming. To make up for that: great cod fishing. Four cod off four lines in four minutes!

Drift in a dinghy over the shallows in Bird Cove to see vast beds of sand dollars, thousands of them crowded together and tipped on edge like round chocolate wafers decorating a cake. The head of Bird Cove is hard to approach on low tides because the bottom shoals so gradually, but try to dig for clams and cockles in the mud flats.

Read Island is sparsely populated and the road is a pair of gravel tracks divided by grass and buttercups. A wonderful walk from the public wharf at Evans Bay to the store at Surge Narrows.[4] About four miles, but it's hard to turn back. The road skirts Bird Cove and then heads inland up, over, and around gentle hills: turning often, and every bend showing something different. Here and there an offshoot trail of tall grass between the trees. A weathered settlement with a driftwood deer-fence. Grown-in pastures; an old orchard. Then miles of nothing but forest that becomes deeper, darker, more primeval mile by mile. The cedars are magnificent. The silence is absolute.

Did you know: That bald eagles are not really bald.

The Makings of a Good Chowder....

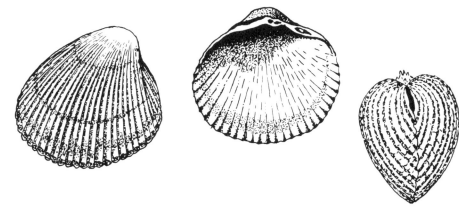

"basket" or "heart" cockle

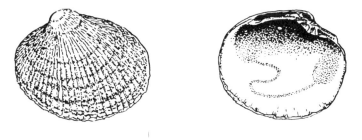

native littleneck clam

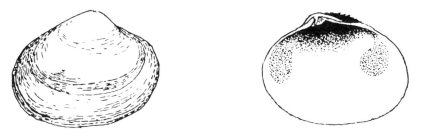

butter clam

Dry bluffs and distant snowfields, Octopus Islands

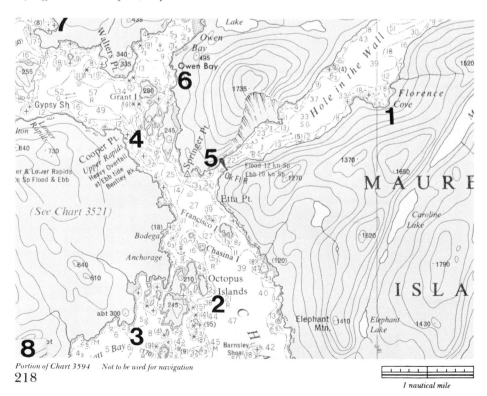

1 nautical mile

50

Hole In The Wall to Waiatt Bay

What's There calm bays and exciting current passages....wildlife and seafood....undeveloped marine park....wilderness shorelines....trails....deserted settlements....

Charts

3521 Okisollo Channel	1:24,000
3594 Discovery Passage, Toba Inlet and connecting channels	1:75,000

Moorage In Florence Cove,[1] temporary anchorage while waiting for slack current in Hole in the Wall. A ledge on the east side of the cove offers space for one or two boats; on the west side kelp makes difficulties in dropping an anchor down to holding ground. During a north wind the cove becomes a "blow-hole": anchor securely.

Among the Octopus Islands[2] and in Waiatt Bay,[3] good anchorage

Facilities None; the closest to Florence Cove, at Stuart Island; and the closest to Octopus Islands, Dodmans Store at Surge Narrows

Octopus Islands Marine Park: undeveloped

Caution Attempt the current passages at Upper and Lower Rapids,[4] at Surge Narrows, and at Hole in the Wall[5] only near slack current. Access to Octopus Islands Marine Park from any direction involves current passages.

Access By boat only

Hole in the Wall is a very narrow breach between islands, all the more impressive because of a steep cliff on one side. When approaching the gap even at slack current you feel that you're being poured down a funnel.

Fast current passages can be exciting. Judge the slack time, and edge forward cautiously. Feel the current take hold, and dodge eddies. Only in the very narrow places, at Upper and Lower Rapids, at Surge Narrows and at Hole in the Wall, does the current demand that you go through only at slack. But even in the wider calmer spaces of Okisollo Channel the water takes directions of its own: mysterious underwellings, like something waiting to come up.

Florence Cove is a convenient waiting place for that elusive slack current, when you approach "the Hole" from the east. A small creek empties over a gravel beach spread with rusty machine pieces and bits of broken crockery. Follow the creek upstream to a clay cutbank: wonderful stuff to get your hands into — a heap of natural plasticine. The old skid roads are so grown in with alder that it's easier to walk through the uncut forest. And you can climb up a bluff where the rocks cushioned with moss make cozy couches.

Okisollo Channel — cruising territory for the venturesome: rapids, cliffs, and wolves howling in the hills. But it can also be an area for serene cruising, with tranquil anchorages, gently-rounded islands, and seals sunning peacefully on the rocks. Fabulous either way.

A good choice of places to pull in and explore. Owen Bay[6] must once have been a busy camp, judging by the shoreline collection of derelict buildings and machines. Barnes Bay[7] is still the site of a logging camp. Octopus Islands, part of a marine park. Some of the property is privately owned, but clearly marked as such. And in Waiatt Bay, good anchorage. The passage between Octopus Islands and the Quadra Island shore: a hallway of water opening into anterooms among the islands, each space large enough to hold a few boats.

You can follow logging roads for miles inland, or walk from Waiatt Bay to Small Inlet across a half-mile neck of land.[8] And you might not catch octopus at Octopus Islands, but you can gather your limit of clams and crabs, and maybe find shrimp inside your crab net. A meal of rock cod within minutes.

Did you know: Sea urchins, those small pincushions found on rocky beaches, many people prize for their roe, as fine as caviar.

Something to Try: Long Walks on Old Roads

Walking is the flip side of cruising, its natural complement, stretching boat-cramped muscles and working off rich meals. And walking is the best way to see what the countryside beyond the shore is all about. Walk along beaches, through towns, across islands, and up mountains, but for long adventurous rambles find old logging roads and long-deserted trails and follow them to their uncharted destinations. Often to abandoned settlements, or waterfalls, or splendid viewpoints, or to lakes with water refreshingly soft to swim in. If nothing else, you'll find berries and other edibles along the way.

A long walk on an isolated route? Go about it in the right way. Weather changes quickly along the coast, so take sunglasses, a light jacket or sweater, some spare socks, and wear a hat or scarf. Accidents can happen, and even short distances have a way of stretching. For spur-of-the-moment walks keep handy a "walking kit" in a light nylon packsack. Just as important, though, are the things you don't take. Keep it light:

> **matches,** in a waterproof container
> **pocket knife**
> **hand compass**
> **bandaids** for blisters
> **plastic bags** to hold collectibles
> container of **hiking food:** raisins, nuts, chocolate....
> **handkerchiefs** for sweatbands, bandages, or , with a knot tied in each corner, for a pirate-style head cover
> large plastic **garbage bags** for ground sheets, emergency cover, or, in a pinch, for rain ponchos

And if you want a boat to come back to, leave it alone only in a very, very secure anchorage.

Stalking clams and cockles

1 nautical mile

51

Kanish Bay

What's There crabs....clams....cockles....wilderness shorelines....settlement ruins....shell middens....old logging machinery....howling wolves....

Charts

3565 Discovery Passage	1:38,000
3594 Discovery Passage, Toba Inlet and connecting channels	1:75,000

Moorage In Granite Bay,[1] a small public landing float used by fish boats

In Kanish Bay[2] and in Small Inlet,[3] anchorage

Facilities None

Nearest complete cruising supplies, at Campbell River, about 15 miles south — but on the other side of Seymour Narrows

Supplies available without going through the Narrows, at Blind Channel on East Thurlow Island: fuel, groceries, accommodation and radiotelephone

Caution Seymour Narrows, more than most current passages along the coast, deserves respect: extreme turbulence, whirlpools and overfalls, and currents up to 14 knots. Consult current tables before attempting this passage.

Access By boat only, to Kanish Bay and to Small Inlet, but car access to Granite Bay by a twisty gravel road

Kanish Bay is a great granite basin with granite islands. No place so silent after dark, and no silence so splendidly shattered by a howling pack of wolves. One thin wail lifting clear of the valley, then others. The whole chorus joining on a ragged note that grows and empties and re-echoes till the night is filled with wailing. Unforgettable.

Kanish Bay is remote without being too far away, for Seymour Narrows draws a gate of fast water across the passage north of Campbell River. The south end of Discovery Passage is busy with tyee fishermen and tourists, the north part mostly left alone except by commercial seine boats. Watch them working in the entrance to Kanish: the fishing must be good here.

Near the entrance to Small Inlet, a cove[4] with good anchorage and a grassy plateau with traces of an old homestead: grass and thistles waist-high under decayed fruit trees, and enormous maples along a creek and over white shell middens.

Between the plateau and anchorage an intertidal seafood paradise: five-inch rock crabs within reach of shore; bushels of cockles found by running your fingers through the sea lettuce. And clams. It's best to rake for clams here because digging breaks too many; keep the broken ones for crab bait and for cod fishing.

Turn to the shallow water at low tide: hermit crabs in borrowed shells; warty sea cucumbers; sea anemones in brilliant shades of orange.

Granite Bay and Small Inlet, the two offshoots of Kanish Bay, are completely different. Granite Bay is civilized: a log dump, some fishboats, a dirt road and a few cabins; a handy place to turn in an emergency. In Small Inlet, rusty piles of logging machinery in the bush, a logging road rising gently inland through logged-open spaces and dark stands of timber across to Waiatt Bay. An eagle plunges down to pick up a fish. A young buck grazes on the foreshore. If wilderness is where wolves howl, then this is surely wilderness.

Did you know: In 1958 the peaks of Ripple Rock, cause of many a shipwreck in Seymour Narrows, were blasted away: the largest man-made, non-atomic explosion in history at the time.

Deserted fields and waist-high grass, Kanish Bay

Index

An asterisk beside a number indicates a photograph.

230

Bibliography

Hundreds of interesting and useful publications related to boating are available. This list includes only those I used most repeatedly while cruising, and found most helpful while writing this book.

ACTIVITIES

Barlee, N.L.	*The Guide to Gold Panning in British Columbia.* Summerland, B.C.: Canada West Publishing, 1972.
Hutchinson, Bill and Hutchinson, Julie.	*Rockhounding and Beachcombing on Vancouver Island.* (2nd ed.) Victoria: Tom and Georgie Vaulkhard, The Rockhound Shop, 1975.
Pratt-Johnson, Betty.	*141 Dives in the protected waters of Washington and British Columbia.* (updated ed.) Vancouver/London: Gordon Soules Book Publishers and Mercer Island, Washington: The Writing Works, Inc., 1977.
Purvis, Ron.	*Treasure Hunting in British Columbia.* Toronto/Montreal: McClelland and Stewart, 1971.
Watson, George and Skrill, Robert.	*Western Canadian Bottle Collecting.* (2 Vols.) Nanaimo, B.C.: The Westward Collector, 1973.

BOATING SKILLS

Andrews, H.L. and Russell, A.L.	*Basic Boating, Piloting and Seamanship.* (rev. ed.) Englewood Cliffs, N.J.: Prentice-Hall, Inc., 1974.
Griffiths, Garth.	*Boating in Canada: Practical Piloting and Seamanship.* (2nd ed.) Toronto: University of Toronto Press, 1971.
Sloane, Gloria and Coe, Phyllis.	*How to Be a First Rate First Mate.* New York: Quadrangle/ The New York Times Co., 1974.

COASTAL PILOTS AND SMALL CRAFT GUIDES

British Columbia:	*British Columbia Small Craft Guide, Volume I: Vancouver Island, Port Alberni to Campbell River including the Gulf Islands.* Ottawa: Canadian Hydrographic Service, Department of the Environment. Updated regularly.
	British Columbia Small Craft Guide, Volume II: Boundary Bay to Cortes Island. Ottawa: Canadian Hydrographic Service, Department of the Environment. Updated regularly.
	Sailing Directions – British Columbia Coast (South Portion). Victoria: Canadian Hydrographic Service, Department of the Environment. Updated about every two years.
Washington:	*United States Coast Pilot 7: Pacific Coast.* Washington, D.C.: Atmospheric Administration/National Ocean Survey. Updated annually.

Arno, Stephen F. and Hammerly, Ramona P.
Northwest Trees. Seattle: The Mountaineers. 1977.

Carl, G.C.
Guide to Marine Life of British Columbia. Victoria: British Columbia Provincial Museum Handbook, No. 21, 1963.
Some Common Marine Fishes. Victoria: British Columbia Provincial Museum Handbook, No. 23, 1971.

Hewlett, Stefani and Hewlett, K.G.
Sea Life of the Pacific Northwest. Toronto: McGraw-Hill Ryerson, 1976.

Kozloff, Eugene N.
Plants and Animals of the Pacific Northwest. Seattle: University of Washington Press, 1976.
Seashore Life of Puget Sound, the Strait of Georgia and the San Juan Archipelago. Seattle: University of Washington Press, 1973

INDIAN ROCK ART

Hill, Beth.
Guide to Indian Rock Carvings of the Pacific Northwest Coast. Saanichton, B.C.: Hancock House, 1975.

Hill, Beth and Hill, Ray.
Indian Petroglyphs of the Pacific Northwest. Saanichton, B.C.: Hancock House, 1974.

Meade, Edward.
Indian Rock Carvings of the Pacific Northwest. Sidney, B.C.: Gray's Publishing Ltd., 1971.

LOCAL GUIDES AND HISTORY: BRITISH COLUMBIA

Antonson, Rick and Trainer, Mary and Antonson, Brian.
In Search of a Legend: Slumach's Gold. New Westminster: Nunaga Publishing Co., 1974.

Calhoun, Bruce.
Mac and the Princess. Seattle: Ricwalt Publishing Co., 1976.

Corrigall, Margery.
Historic Hornby Island. (rev. ed.) Courtenay, B.C.: Comox District Free Press, 1975.

Hamilton, Bea.
Salt Spring Island. Vancouver: Mitchell Press Ltd., 1969.

Howard, Irene.
Bowen Island, 1872 - 1972. (2nd ed.) Bowen Island, B.C.: Bowen Island Historians, 1973.

Mason, Elda Copley.
Lasqueti Island: History and Memory. South Wellington, B.C.: Mrs. Elda Maria Mason, 1976.

Pattison, Ken.
Milestones on Vancouver Island. (2nd ed.) Victoria: Milestone Publications, 1974.

Peterson, Lester R.
The Gibson's Landing Story. Toronto: Peter Martin Associates Ltd., 1962.

Rogers, Fred.
Shipwrecks of the British Columbia Coast. Vancouver: J.J. Douglas Ltd., 1973.

Rushton, Gerald A.
Whistle Up the Inlet: the Union Steamship Story. Vancouver: J.J. Douglas Ltd., 1978.

CRUISE GUIDEBOOKS

Berssen, William.
Pacific Boating Almanac. Ventura, California: Western Marine Enterprises, Inc. Revised annually.

Blanchet, M. Wylie.
The Curve of Time. (3rd ed.) Sidney, B.C.: Gray's Publishing Ltd., 1977.

Calhoun, Bruce.	*Cruising the San Juan Islands.* Newfoundland, New Jersey: SEA/Haessner Publishing, Inc., 1973. *Northwest Passages: A Collection of Northwest Cruising Stories, Volume I.* (updating footnotes) Ventura, California: Western Marine Enterprises, Inc., 1978. *Northwest Passages: A Collection of Northwest Cruising Stories, Volume II.* Newfoundland, New Jersey: SEA/Haessner Publishing, Inc., 1972.
Dawson, Will.	*Coastal Cruising.* (3rd enl. ed.) Vancouver: Mitchell Press Ltd., 1965.
Hilson, Stephen.	*Exploring Puget Sound and British Columbia.* (enl. ed.) Holland, Michigan: Van Winkle Publishing Co., 1976.
Wolferstan, Bill.	*Pacific Yachting's Cruising Guide to the Gulf Islands and Vancouver Island from Sooke to Courtenay.* Vancouver: Pacific Yachting, Interpress Publications Ltd., 1976.

FISHING AND FORAGING

Bandoni, R.J. and Szczawinski, A.F.	*Guide to Common Mushrooms of British Columbia.* (rev. ed.) Victoria: British Columbia Provincial Museum Handbook, No. 24, 1976.
Challenger, Jean.	*How to Cook Your Catch!* (2nd rev. ed.) Sidney, B.C.: Saltaire Publishing Co., 1977.
Cramond, Mike.	*Fishin' Holes of the West.,* Vancouver: Mitchell Press, 1972.
Furlong, Marjorie and Pill, Virginia.	*Edible? Incredible!* (4th ed.) Tacoma, Washington: Erco, Inc., 1976.
Gibbons, Euell.	*Stalking the Blue-Eyed Scallop.* (field guide ed.) New York: David McKay Co., Inc., 1970.
Haw, Frank and Buckley, Raymond M.	*Saltwater Fishing in Washington.* Seattle: Stan Jones Publishing, Inc., 1973.
Jackson, Ainley	*Vancouver Aquarium Seafood Recipes.* Vancouver/London: Gordon Soules Book Publishers and Mercer Island, Wash.: The Writing Works, Inc., 1977.
Madlener, Judith Cooper.	*The Sea Vegetable Book: Foraging and Cooking Seaweed.* New York: Clarkson N. Potter, Inc., 1977.
McKenny, Margaret.	*The Savory Wild Mushroom.* (rev. and enl. ed. edited by Daniel E. Stuntz) Seattle/London: University of Washington Press, 1976.
Members of the Puget Sound Mycological Society.	*Wild Mushroom Recipes.* Seattle: Pacific Search Press, 1973.
Mohney, Russ.	*The Dogfish Cookbook.* Sidney, B.C.: Gray's Publishing Ltd. and Seattle: Pacific Search Press, 1976.
Szczawinski, A.F. and Hardy, G.A.	*Guide to Common Edible Plants of British Columbia.* Victoria: British Columbia Provincial Museum Handbook, No. 20, 1962.
Underhill, J.E.	*Wild Berries of the Pacific Northwest.* Saanichton, B.C.: Hancock House Publishers, 1974.
White, Charles.	*How to Catch Bottomfish!* Sidney, B.C.: Saltaire Publishing Ltd., 1974. (and several other fish and shellfish topics in the "How To" series by this publisher.)

Burke, E. and others — *San Juan Islands Almanac*. Friday Harbor, Washington: Long House Printcrafters, 1977.

Kellogg, George A. — *A History of Whidbey's Island*. Seattle: Shorey Publications, 1968.

Murray, Keith A. — *The Pig War*. Tacoma, Washington: Washington State Historical Society, 1968.

Richardson, David B. — *Pig War Islands*. Eastsound, Washington: Orcas Publishing Company, 1971.

Williamson, Joe and Gibbs, Jim. — *Maritime Memories of Puget Sound*. Seattle: Superior Publishing Company, 1976.

Willis, Margaret, editor. — *Chechacos All: The Pioneering of Skagit*. Skagit County Historical Series No. 3. Mount Vernon, Washington: Skagit County Historical Society, 1973.

PLACE NAMES

Akrigg, G.P.V. and Akrigg, Helen B. — *1001 Place Names in B.C.* (3rd rev. ed.) Vancouver: Discovery Press, 1973.

Meany, Edmond S. — *Origin of Washington Geographic Names*. Detroit: Gale Research Company, 1968.

Middleton, Lyn. — *Place Names of the Pacific Northwest Coast*. Victoria: Elldee Publishing, 1969.

Phillips, James W. — *Washington State Place Names*. (rev. and enl. ed.) Seattle and London: University of Washington Press, 1976.

Walbran, John T. — *British Columbia Coast Names, 1592 - 1906*. Vancouver: J.J. Douglas, 1971.

MAGAZINES AND PERIODICALS

Beautiful British Columbia. (quarterly) British Columbia Department of Travel Industry, Parliament Buildings, Victoria.

Directory of British Columbia Tourist Accommodation. (annually) Tourism British Columbia, Ministry of the Provincial Secretary and Travel Industry, 1117 Wharf Street, Victoria, B.C.

Northwest Boat Travel. (quarterly) Post Office Box 1147, Mount Vernon, Washington.

Northwest Experience: Washington State Outdoor Recreation Guide. (quarterly) Northwest Experience Publishing Co., 409 South Jackson St., Moscow, Idaho.

Northwest Sea. (monthly) CBS Publications, 600 Third Avenue, New York, N.Y.

Pacific Yachting – Power and Sail. (monthly) Interpress Publications Ltd., #202-1132 Hamilton St., Vancouver, B.C.

Raincoast Chronicles. (quarterly) Harbour Publishing, Box 119, Madeira Park, B.C.

CREDITS

Photographs:
Doug Nealy: front cover
Bill Gregory: page 24
Government of B.C.: page 88
Michael Van der Ree: back cover
All other photographs are by the author.

Drawings: Philip J. Croft
Maps: John Winfield, Altair Drafting Services, Ltd.

Books Recommended by
Gordon Soules Book Publishers Ltd.